AROUND

bOston

WITH KIDS

2nd Edition

by Lisa Oppenheimer

Fodor's Travel Publications
New York • Toronto • London • Sydney • Auckland

www.fodors.com

CREDITS

Writer: Lisa Oppenheimer

Series Editors: Karen Cure, Andrea Lehman
Editor: Andrea Lehman
Editorial Production: Tom Holton
Production/Manufacturing: Bob Shields

Design: Fabrizio La Rocca, creative director;
Tigist Getachew, art director
Illustration and Series Design: Rico Lins, Keren Ora
Admoni/Rico Lins Studio

ABOUT THE WRITER

Lisa Oppenheimer, mother of two, is a contributor to *Disney* and *Parents* magazines as well as family travel columnist for Fodors.com. Lisa is also the author of *Fodor's Around Los Angeles with Kids*.

FODOR'S AROUND BOSTON WITH KIDS

Second Edition
ISBN 1–4000–1065–9
ISSN 1531–3349

IMPORTANT TIP

Although all prices, opening times, and other details in this book are based on information supplied to us at press time, changes occur all the time in the travel world, and Fodor's cannot accept responsibility for facts that become outdated or for inadvertent errors or omissions. So always confirm information when it matters, especially if you're making a detour to visit a specific place.

SPECIAL SALES

Fodor's Travel Publications are available at special discounts for bulk purchases for sales promotions or premiums. Special editions, including personalized covers, excerpts of existing guides, and corporate imprints, can be created in large quantities for special needs. For more information, contact your local bookseller or Special Markets, Fodor's Travel Publications, 1745 Broadway, New York, NY 10019. Inquiries from Canada should be directed to your local Canadian bookseller or sent to Random House of Canada, Ltd., Marketing Dept., 2775 Matheson Boulevard East, Mississauga, Ontario L4W 4P7. Inquiries from the United Kingdom should be sent to Fodor's Travel Publications, 20 Vauxhall Bridge Road, London, England SW1V 2SA.

PRINTED IN THE UNITED STATES OF AMERICA
10 9 8 7 6 5 4 3 2 1

COUNTDOWN TO GOOD TIMES!

GET READY, GET SET!

Boston's a city of many images. Devoted sports fans know it for its fabled Bruins and Celtics, hard-luck Sox, and champion Patriots. TV viewers know it for lovably kooky barflies and a little bar where everybody knows your name. But Boston's contemporary icons aren't the only images in town. Gridiron players share the spotlight with those *other* patriots, Colonial-era statesmen who helped to spark the American Revolution.

Beantown's historical notoriety is a big part of the city, something it wears as a badge of honor. Numerous odes to the city's past are enmeshed in the region's present, from the building where colonists plotted the Boston Tea Party to the very spot where some of the first shots of the revolution were fired. Investigating is fun. History Hub-style might mean biking the path of the Minutemen, climbing in the footsteps of the man who signaled Paul Revere for his famous ride, or joining an "uprising" just like the Boston Tea Party. Spring and summer finds famous patriots like Ben Franklin and Paul Revere "reincarnated" as tour guides. And, there's more—from museums to art, sports, theater, and academia.

What follows is a list of 68 of our favorite things to do in the area. Some are educational, some are physically challenging, and some are fun just for the sake of fun. Still, it's a big region with enough attractions to fill volumes. Fans of the stage can find national touring shows in the theater district as well as family fare from the Wheelock Family Theatre, among others. Look for old-fashioned weekend entertainment at Brookline's Coolidge Corner Theater's Kids Variety Saturdays. Walk downtown and you can't help but peer into the underground world of Boston's Big Dig. The truly curious might even be able to get on a tour (for maps and info, try www.bigdig.com/thtml/dod_tour.htm). After a long renovation, the Mapparium, a dramatic walk-through glass globe at the Mary Baker Eddy Library of the Boston Christian Science Center (200 Massachusetts Ave., tel. 617/450-7300; www.marybakereddylibrary.org) has reopened. Don't-miss seasonal staples include First Night (New Year's Eve), the Boston Marathon (April), the Boston Ballet's Nutcracker at the Wang Center (roughly Thanksgiving through early January), and concerts on the Common and at the Hatch Shell.

Additional favorites outside the city include the charming Wenham Museum (132 Main St., Wenham, tel. 978/468-2377) and the New Bedford Whaling Museum (18 Johnny Cake Hill, New Bedford, tel. 508/997-0046). And never let it be said that New England isn't a little quirky, with such gems as the American Sanitary Plumbing Museum (39 Piedmont St., Worcester, tel. 508/754-9453), National Plastics Center and Museum (210 Lancaster St., Leominster, tel. 978/537-9529), and Museum of Dirt (36 Drydock St., South Boston).

RESOURCES
Even if you live in Massachusetts, it pays to gather information like a tourist. A good place to start is the Greater Boston Convention & Visitors Bureau (tel. 888/SEE-BOSTON, www.bostonusa.com). If you're in the city, stop by the bureau's visitor centers, located at the Boston Common and the Prudential Center.

HOW TO SAVE MONEY

We list only regular adult and child prices; children under the ages specified are free. It always pays to ask at the ticket booth whether any discounts are offered for a particular status (such as seniors) or affiliation (such as AAA). Don't forget to bring your ID. Family memberships at many attractions include free admission and usually pay for themselves if you visit the attraction several times a year. If you like a place when you visit, you can often apply the value of your one-day admission to a membership if you do it before you leave.

Look for coupons—everywhere from the local newspaper to a supermarket display, your pediatrician's office and the Visitors Bureau. Some places offer frequent-visitor cards that give a free or discounted admission with a specified number of paid admissions. Also, keep an eye out for attractions—mostly museums and other cultural destinations—that offer free admission one day a month or one day a week after a certain time. We've noted several in this book.

Boston's CityPass offers discounted admission to six attractions: the Harvard Museum of Natural History, John F. Kennedy Library and Museum, Museum of Fine Arts, Museum of Science, New England Aquarium, and Prudential Center Skywalk. Passes, which must be used within nine days, can be purchased at one of the attractions, through the Greater Boston Convention & Visitors Bureau or its visitor centers, or at www.citypass.net.

WHEN TO GO AND HOW TO GET THERE

With the exception of seasonal attractions, kid-oriented destinations are generally busiest when children are out of school—especially weekends, holidays, and summer—but not necessarily. Attractions that draw school and camp trips can be swamped on a midweek morning. But such groups tend to leave by early afternoon, so weekdays after 2 can be excellent times to visit. For outdoor attractions, it's good to show up after a rain, since crowds tend to clear out. The hours listed in this book are an attraction's basic hours, not necessarily those applicable on holidays. It's always best to call ahead.

If you're traveling outside the city, you'll likely have to drive, although a growing number of trains run through some of the 'burbs. You'll definitely want to devise your schedule around Boston's notorious rush hour, which actually spans roughly 7–9 in the morning and 3:30–6:30 in the evening. Driving in rush-hour traffic can be maddening, but even off-peak car travel can be exasperating. Downtown roads are a veritable maze, where all streets seem to be one-way. Highways? Where else can you find a road on which you can travel north and south at the same time? Even if that doesn't confuse you, the havoc wreaked by the Big Dig (rumor has it it will be done some day) probably will. And then, there's parking.

In and immediately around the city, opt for public buses, trolleys, and subways, otherwise known as the "T." The fare is currently $1, with surcharges outside the city. If you're coming inbound, however, beware that parking at the outlying stations is often a challenge, particularly on weekdays. Subway riders can purchase tokens on site, but above ground, you'll need exact change. Visitor Passes can be purchased for one, three, and seven days and include unlimited travel on subways, local buses, and inner harbor ferries. Residents can purchase weekly and monthly passes for subways, commuter rail, or a combination of both. Bikes are welcomed on a limited basis; check the MBTA's site (www.MBTA.com) for details.

HOW TO USE THIS BOOK

Attractions are arranged alphabetically and numbered in reverse order (like a countdown)—from 68 to 1—and do not reflect any preference or rating. Info at the top details the basics: address, phone, Web site, prices, hours, and suggested ages. Look for other particulars—where to eat, nearby and related activities, and fun facts for kids—in the boxes. If you want to search for sights based on geography or subject matter, flip to the directories at the back of the book. And speaking of flipping, don't forget to create your own lobster movie magic by looking in the bottom right corner while you flip the pages.

After you've explored a bit, let us know what you think. If you happened upon a place that you think warrants a mention, by all means, send it along. You can e-mail us at editors@fodors.com (specify Around Boston with Kids on the subject line), or write to us at Around Boston with Kids, Fodor's Travel Publications, 1745 Broadway, New York, NY 10019. We'll put your ideas to good use. In the meantime, have fun!

—Lisa Oppenheimer

ARCHERY USA

68

Given the dearth of archers with sneaker endorsements, it's no surprise that most kids know little about this ages-old sport. But once they get going, children are drawn in by the challenge of trying to hit that little gold circle with a tiny arrowhead, especially since the hand-eye coordination required rivals that of most video games. In fact, it can get downright addictive.

Visitors to the indoor facility are first sized up to determine their shooting arm. First-time William Tells might be surprised to find that they're instructed to pull the string with their non-favored arm. Actually, your shooting stance is determined not by your dominant hand but by your dominant eye, which is easily tested on the spot. Everyone is then equipped with beginner bows and sent on to the range. Standing behind the green line, you fire at a target 20 yards away. Several targets are adjustable, so young children (or their parents!) can have it moved close enough for some arrows to find their mark. Once on deck, pay close attention to the four commands shouted (LOUDLY!) during the session: "On-line"

HEY, KIDS! When you think of precision engineering, you probably don't think of the good ol' bow and arrow. So you might be surprised that top Olympic archers routinely buy high-tech bows that cost thousands of dollars. Made of carbon compounds, these bows are engineered to withstand the pounding and vibrations that pros subject them to. Carbon arrows—designed for maximum aerodynamics (to fly faster and straighter)—are also extremely expensive. Needless to say, you're going to have to practice on the Chevy bow for a while before you can graduate to the Mercedes-Benz.

606 Providence Hwy.
(Rte. 1 northbound), Dedham

781/320-3606;
www.archeryusa.com

 $8 per hr ages 16
and up, $6 per hr
children 15 and under;
equipment $5 per hr

 T-F 1-9, Sa-Su 1-6

 7 and up

(get into position), "Begin" (load bow and shoot), "Hold" (bring the string back to original position), and "Let Down" (an emergency command to stop what you're doing). This protocol is in place to ensure that no one fires while anyone is retrieving arrows (and vice versa).

According to owner Anthony Bellettini, children make up a large portion of archers here—about 6,000–8,000 kids a year. Part of the draw is the goal: to achieve a personal best rather than to trounce your rival. The ultimate achievement, called a Robin Hood, entails shooting an arrow into the back of another arrow already in the target's center. (Don't get your hopes up!)

For obvious reasons, Archery USA runs a tight (and strict) ship—no horsing around and no running. No one, after all, wants to come off the range looking like Steve Martin in one of his old comedy routines.

EATS FOR KIDS
T.G.I. Friday's (750 Providence Hwy., tel. 781/251–0650), next door, offers plentiful, tasty chain fare, plus crayons. For more homespun atmosphere, try the family-owned **Midway Restaurant** (269 Washington St., tel. 781/329–5575), whose vast menu includes seafood and salads as well as children's favorites.

KEEP IN MIND With 20 lanes, Archery USA usually has some open, but big groups should reserve ahead. Staff here is certified, trained, licensed, and insured by the National Archery Association, the organization that runs the sport nationwide and selects teams for national and Olympic competition. To really improve, sign up for the 1½-hour classes (all ages). Classes (roughly $13 each) are offered Friday 7–8:30 and Saturday 9–10:30 and 11–12:30. Though students typically register for six weeks, drop-ins (to try it out) are often accommodated. Children 16 and under must be accompanied by a parent at all times.

ARNOLD ARBORETUM

67

If the words "Botanical Garden" make you think "stuffy," think again. How stuffy can it really be if you can career around it on a pair of Rollerblades?

An unusual partnership between the folks at Harvard University and the Boston Parks and Recreation Department, this arboretum (founded in 1872) combines science with recreation, allowing visitors to appreciate the workings of the botanical world as well as its inherent pleasures. At 265 acres, the vast sweep of greenery is an unlikely surprise, particularly since it's tucked inside citified Jamaica Plain and its apartment houses and office buildings.

More than 13,000 labeled trees, shrubs, and other plants cover the acreage here, with something in bloom nearly all the time from February through late November. December and January are pretty blooming quiet, but then, who wants to walk in the winter cold anyway? Notable inhabitants include the Seven-Son Flower, an Asian plant that exists

HEY, KIDS!
Like animals, plant seeds have survival strategies. Maple seeds have "wings" to carry them away from the mother tree's shade. Willow trees produce seeds early in spring, when it's wet enough for them to sprout. As for fruit seeds, let's just say they're, er, distributed via animals' digestive systems.

EATS FOR KIDS The arboretum is within walking distance of all of the restaurants of downtown Jamaica Plain. One good choice is the **Centre Street Cafe** (669 Centre St., tel. 617/524–9217), where a world of foods from Tex-Mex to Asian features mostly organic ingredients. Dishes can be prepared to meet vegetarian needs. You'll need either a car or bike to get to **Doyle's** (3484 Washington St., tel. 617/524–2345), but the longtime neighborhood haunt's combination of pub fare and entrées is worth the trip.

125 Arborway (off Jamaica Way), Jamaica Plain

617/524–1718; www.arboretum.harvard.edu

 Donations accepted

 Daily sunrise–sunset; Hunnewell Building, Apr–Oct, M–F 9–4, Sa–Su 12–4; Nov–Mar, Sa–Su 10–2 (sometimes closed in Jan)

All ages

in only a few places in this country. The bonsai are usually a big hit with kids (look for them mid-April–mid-November); some of these tiny little trees date from the mid-18th century. Indoor educational exhibits at the Hunnewell Building (including a few that are interactive) are worth a visit.

The genus and species of Arnold's plant life probably won't bowl younger children over. "Look, Mommy, pretty flowers!" is about the best you can hope for. Still, bright colors and wide-open spaces are definite attention grabbers, but don't forget to look where you're going if you're taking in the sights on a set of wheels (i.e., skates or bikes). Paved paths run for roughly 1½ miles around the grounds and are generally car free (vehicles require a special permit). That, paired with the mostly flat terrain, makes this place so safe it's become a haven for first-time bladers. There are a couple of hills, most notably Peter's Hill, from which you can get some great views of the Boston skyline.

KEEP IN MIND Since trees are part of the scientific collection, tree climbing and ball playing (both of which might damage these centuries-old marvels) are strictly prohibited. Picnicking is also a no-no. The arboretum's biggest event is Lilac Sunday, held in mid-May. People have been coming since the turn of the 20th century to see the 400 lilacs (about 200 different kinds) in bloom. It's also the only day of the year when you're allowed to picnic. In addition, the event features entertainment and food vendors.

F ace it. Not all of us can be a genius with a glue gun or rival our children's school art teachers in ability and inspiration. Thankfully, there are some talented folks willing to share their knack for artistry at ArtBeat, an art supply store that offers open studio hours every afternoon. Here you and your little ones can dabble in spur-of-the-moment creative exploits together and—the best part for kids—play with some messy mixtures they might not get to touch at home.

Projects take from about 45 minutes to an hour. Look for decoupage (a type of glazed collage), doll making, candle making, picture frames, and more. Sometimes you'll get to choose from a list. At other times (mainly during school vacations, when the studio tends to get busy), you'll be guided by a theme.

Younger artists (starting at age 4) might appreciate some adult input, but staffers caution parents not to help too much. (The studio can't work with children under 4, but staff members

EATS FOR KIDS If you're up for a tasty gastronomic adventure, try the Lebanese specialties of **Cafe Barada** (201 Massachusetts Ave., tel. 781/646–9650). The yogurt–cucumber salad is a big hit, and kids have been known to like the kebabs. Go to the Italian/Mediterranean **Neillio's** (218 Massachusetts Ave., tel. 781/643–6644) for absolutely wonderful fresh pastas—fettuccine, ravioli, and many others—with sauces to match.

212A Massachusetts Ave., East Arlington

 $8–$15

781/646-2200; www.artbeatonline.com

 Studio hrs M–F 11–5, Sa–Su 3–5

4 and up

will help you assemble materials to coach little ones in the featured craft at home.) Older children, on the other hand, might prefer to work independently. If that's the case, consider pulling up a chair and doing a project of your own.

For those who fear an art workshop more than the auto repair shop, fear not. There's no pressure to produce a Picasso. Owner Jan Whitted stresses that ability is secondary to desire. "You're free to be a beginner," she says. The ArtBeat atmosphere is homey, and instructors are pleasant. Their aim is just to spark your family's imagination enough so you enjoy the experience and perhaps continue flexing your creative muscles on your own.

HEY, KIDS! Challenge yourself by trying something completely different. Even if the activity of the day is painting, you don't have to stick to the same old routine. Staff members will be happy to show you some different painting techniques, such as sponging, dry brushing, or stenciling.

KEEP IN MIND Though the store itself is open much of each day, studio hours are limited, and you must arrive at least an hour before the studio's closing to take part in a craft. Occasionally, a few slots open up before 3 on weekends, so if you're feeling the urge to create then, give a call. In fact, it's a good idea to call ahead for reservations at all times, since the studio is small.

BATTLESHIP COVE

65

Every war produces military legends, but few are bigger—in the purely literal sense—than World War II's "Big Mamie." Mamie, as it happens, is not a "who" but a "what"—the enormous Battleship *Massachusetts,* nicknamed Mamie by her crew. The vessel currently resides at Battleship Cove, part of a stationary fleet assembled as a memorial to Massachusetts residents who died in combat.

For kids, this is pay dirt in the naval history and adventuring department. Several floating monuments—in addition to Mamie, the military craft here include the U.S.S. *Joseph P. Kennedy, Jr.,* a destroyer; two PT boats; and a submarine—are open for exploration. (There's also a Vietnam War–era helicopter and a Japanese suicide boat, but you'll have to appreciate those from the outside only.) Wander through Mamie from top to nearly bottom, examining the engine room, poking around crew quarters, and even positioning the artillery (you can aim some of the battleship's 40-mm guns, but you can't fire them). The 690-foot ship seems large until you realize it accommodated more than 2,000 sailors at a time.

HEY, KIDS!
Just how big is the *Massachusetts?* This sturdy lady is as long as two football fields, and, if she were on land, she would stand taller than four two-story homes stacked on top of one another. How much does she weigh? Oh, a mere 46,000 tons.

KEEP IN MIND The Battleship Cove community also includes summer sailboat rental through Community Boating (able sailors only; others will have to take instruction) as well as an antique carousel (tel. 508/678–1100 or 508/324–4345 for both). The adjacent Heritage State Park (200 Davol St., tel. 508/675–5759) has a visitor center with cultural exhibits. Other local sights include the Marine Museum (70 Water St., tel. 508/674–3533), and the Old Colony & Fall River Railroad Museum (tel. 508/674–9340), which is closed in winter.

Rte. 24 Exit 7, Fall River

 508/678–1100 or 800/533–3194; www.battleshipcove.org

 $10 ages 15 and up, $5 children 6–14

 Apr–June, daily 9–5; July–early Sept, daily 9–5:30; mid-Sept–Mar, daily 9–4:30

All ages

That's nothing next to the cramped quarters of the submarine *Lionfish*. Roam the confines of this 311-foot underwater tube, and imagine sharing it with 81 grown men. It'll remind you that none of these ladies was built to be glamorous, but neither are they personality-less hulls. They have enormous sentimental value, particularly to those who manned them more than a half century ago. On many days you'll find devoted former crew members aboard Mamie just to give her a lovingly applied spit shine.

Though most visitors are day-trippers, Mamie hosts a large number of overnighters as well. Most are school and scout groups, but families can join in if there's room—just give a call. You'll get to sleep in the same battleship quarters the crew slept in (assuming you consider this a good thing!), but you'll enjoy a much better "mess" of chicken, mashed potatoes, and gravy (breakfast and lunch are included, too).

EATS FOR KIDS You can get onboard chow (hot dogs, hamburgers, clam chowder, and the like) at the **snack bar.** (You can also bring your own food as long as you eat it in the snack bar area.) If you want to eat off the ship, try **Applebee's Neighborhood Grill** (311 Plymouth Ave., tel. 508/675–1110), where the grub includes salads, sandwiches, soups, and a kids' menu.

BLUE HILLS TRAILSIDE MUSEUM
AND RESERVATION

For such a cosmopolitan city, Boston is surrounded by a surprising amount of open space. Case in point: the Blue Hills Reservation. This giant slice of the great outdoors is positively Eden-like. You'll never believe you're only 10 miles from the city.

At 7,000 acres, the reservation is a vast hunk of nature. More than 150 miles of trails crisscross the place, providing terrain for explorers on mountain bikes or on foot. (In-line skaters are out of luck as there are no paved paths.) The highest elevations provide some striking views.

But all that's just the beginning. Winter warriors can speed downhill on the slopes at the Blue Hills Ski Area (4001 Washington St., Canton, tel. 781/828–5070) or enjoy the reservation's trails cross-country style. Warm-weather wanderers can refresh themselves with a dip in Houghton's Pond. Year-round you can get in the saddle and mosey the trails on horseback (see below).

EATS FOR KIDS On the edge of the reservation, you can get home cookin' at **Newcomb Farms** (1139 Randolph Ave., tel. 617/698–9547). The cozy place serves brunch dishes as well as tasty sandwiches, grills, salads, and just about anything else you can think of. Though decidedly less homey, the **99 Restaurant and Pub** (162 Turnpike St., Canton, tel. 781/821–8999), less than 2 miles away, also serves grills, sandwiches, and salads and the ever-essential kids' menu.

Nature lovers can learn a little more about the area at the on-site Blue Hills Trailside Museum. Appropriately named (it is indeed next to the trails), the small facility is, in effect, a scaled-down version of the reservation, representing the park's different habitats, including woodland, pond, and wetland. A few nifty indoor features include a natural honey factory (AKA a beehive—windows let you watch the action) and a full-size Wetu, a bark structure once used by Massachusetts Indians. The museum's outdoor acreage—16 acres in all—includes a self-guided pond walk and a number of animal enclosures. For an optimal afternoon, start your adventure at the museum, where you can park and purchase an all-important map. Spend the rest of the day wending your way around the trails. Those who skip the inside exhibits don't have to miss out on the museum completely. Animal habitats for white-tailed deer, river otters, red-tailed hawks, and other animals are open even when the museum isn't and can be viewed free of charge.

HEY, KIDS! Wonder why there are stone walls in the Blue Hills woods? They were property boundaries, built by 18th-century farmers. Blue Hills is actually what's called a second-growth forest. Most of the original trees were cleared for farming in the late 1700s. Miraculously, the forest has rejuvenated itself, thanks to nature's reseeding.

KEEP IN MIND Make sure to ask about the museum's numerous programs, including Maple Sugar Days (March) and school-vacation events. As for horseback riding, the St. Moritz stable (629 Willard St., Quincy, tel. 617/472–0649) offers year-round trail rides for those aged 12 and up. The cost is $40 per hour. Call for hours and the necessary reservations. Please note: trails are for walking; no trotting, etc., is allowed.

BOSTON BY SEA

63

Boston has made a cottage industry out of historic walking tours. Unfortunately, some of the city's most history-rich territory—that lying offshore in the Boston Harbor—is a bit hard to stroll around on your own. Luckily, the folks at the Boston History Collaborative have created the next best thing: a lively 90-minute presentation that details hundreds of years of Boston maritime facts. Staged on a three-level harbor cruiser, the show uses live performers, video, and the scenery outside your window to chronicle the harbor's role in history.

Two actors with a trunk full of props run the show. In addition to spinning yarns and singing songs, the pair channel a cast of bygone characters (a nautical "powder monkey" and a pirate, among them) seemingly with the change of a hat. Guests—particularly young ones—can quite literally be swept into the action as these tireless thespians concoct their stories. It's an engaging way to learn a thing or two. The concept—to paint a picture of what the harbor used to look like—is a little like the landlocked Old Town

HEY, KIDS!
Want to be a pirate? Late in the show, young visitors are recruited to unfurl the Jolly Roger (the black skull and crossbones flag that commonly flew on pirate ships) and cavort around the decks with Calico Jack. Your reward for your efforts is a bit of pirate booty: candy.

KEEP IN MIND Tours leave from Rowes Wharf rain or shine, and indoor seating (there's outdoor seating, too) makes this a nifty rainy-day activity. On the other hand, wet weather often means bumpy seas—bad news for those prone to seasickness. Most of the performance takes place inside on the boat's second level, but the narration is audible throughout. Seats on the port side give you the best look at sights as they are being described by the actors. As always, dress for your destination. Temperature on the water can be a lot cooler than on land, so bring your trusty sweater.

Mass Bay Line, Rowes Wharf, behind Boston Harbor Hotel

$24.99 ages 13 and up, $15.99 children 6–12

617/542–8000; www.bostonbysea.org

May–mid-June and early Sept–mid-Oct, Sa–Su 2; mid-June–early Sept, daily 12 and 2

5 and up

Trolley tours (see #18), except that you can't (or shouldn't) get on and off along the way. Even that may change in the future, as organizers ponder ways to team up with some attractions.

Tours include lots of information—too much for anyone to absorb all at once—but the content has been designed to allow you to walk in and out without feeling that you've fallen behind. Details range from the significance of the "Golden Stairs" (where many New England–bound immigrants first set foot on American soil) to the harbor's previous designation as a "toilet" (the once filthy water is much cleaner these days thanks to concerted effort). Other sights along the way include George's Island, Boston Light, Castle Island, and the U.S.S. *Constitution* (see listings for each). An extra perk for budding aviators: you'll pass close enough to the airport to want to duck when those jumbo jets make their approaches.

EATS FOR KIDS Soft drinks, snacks, and box lunches (likely a sandwich, chips, etc., but exact contents TBD) are served at the onboard **snack bar.** If you're happy by the water, grab a picnic and enjoy the view at the end of Rowes Wharf. If you've got a craving for Italian, try Faneuil Hall's **Il Panino** (120 South Market Faneuil Hall, tel. 617/573–9700), where you can make yourself happy with some great salads, pastas, and risottos and make the kids happy with tasty pizzas. And of course, the vast number of other Quincy Market eateries are also at your disposal (see #38).

BOSTON COMMON

The first thing you need to know about this public park is that it's called the "Common" (singular), as opposed to the "Commons" (plural). The savannah of Boston's urban jungle for more than three centuries, the Common started out in the 1600s as a communal grazing ground for local farm cows (hence the name). The pastoral image was sorely tainted by the advent of public hangings and floggings, not to mention the encampment of British soldiers during the Revolutionary War. Thankfully, today's pastimes are more sanguine.

Despite various efforts to divide and sell it (and the no-doubt salacious glances from private developers), the Common has endured as public property. Today it maintains its status as the city's gathering ground, as evidenced by such noteworthy 20th-century events as a speech by Martin Luther King, Jr., and a visit by the Pope.

Still, causes are not required to congregate. On these 48 acres in the middle of the city, there's plenty of room to simply throw a ball or push a stroller, all the while breathing in

KEEP IN MIND Frog Pond Ice Skating (tel. 617/635–2120) usually starts the first week in November and goes through mid-March (Sunday–Thursday 10–9, Friday–Saturday 10–10). Concerts and special events are often held on the Common. Call the Boston Parks and Recreation Department (tel. 617/635–4505) for information about them as well as about the annual summer Shakespeare on the Common.

Visitor center, 147 Tremont St.

 Free

Daily sunrise–sunset

888/733–2678, 617/635–7383 Boston
Park Rangers; www.cityofboston.gov

All ages

fresh air. Climbing, sliding, and playing in the sand are the inherent joys of the good-size playground. Shallow Frog Pond—neither a real pond nor a home for frogs—lures thousands of kids to cool off in its fountain each summer. In winter, when Frog freezes over, the place (albeit in diminutive form) becomes to Boston what the Rockefeller Center ice rink is to New York.

History buffs can scope out the park's historical significance by perusing some of the landmarks. Monuments include the Boston Massacre Memorial, created in 1888 by Robert Kraus, and the Shaw Memorial, an 1897 structure honoring the Union Army's first free black regiment. The centuries-old Central Burying Ground is also here.

EATS FOR KIDS
Up in the theater district, **Bennigan's** (191 Stuart St., tel. 617/227–3754) boasts the large chain menu we all know and love, plus tools for coloring. Also see an option under Swan Boats at the Public Garden.

HEY, KIDS! Check out this 17th-century English in a city proclamation: "Noe comon marish and Pastur Ground shall herafter bye gifte or sayle, exchange, or otherwise, be counted unto property without consent of ye major part of ye inhabitants of ye towne." In 21st-century terms, it forbade the sale of any of the Common's grounds.

BOSTON DUCK TOURS

61

One if by land, two if by sea, three if by...Duck. OK, it's not exactly Longfellow, but Boston Duck Tours actually take you by land *and* by sea (or at least the Charles River). Don't confuse these tours with the Make Way for Ducklings Tour (*see* #27). These "Ducks" are an actual mode of transportation, namely authentic WWII amphibious vehicles currently used as tour buses. The fleet of 17 steel waders spirit visitors around Boston, first on terra firma and eventually heading down the ramp near the Museum of Science to end up afloat (by design, of course) in the Charles. If the idea of touring historic Boston doesn't excite your kids, these quirky contraptions, which look like a cross between a military truck and a jungle boat, almost certainly will.

Tours last roughly 80–90 minutes. Along the way, Ducks waddle by important Boston sights and neighborhoods, including Beacon Hill, downtown Boston, and several sights

EATS FOR KIDS There's plenty of Italian food at **Vinny Testa's** (867 Boylston St., tel. 617/262–6699). Among the dozens of restaurants in the Prudential Center are the soups, salads, and such at **Rebecca's Cafe** (*see* #14).

KEEP IN MIND Ducks are open-air vehicles, covered only by a canopy. Plastic side shields are lowered in cool or rainy weather, but you'll still be exposed to the elements, so dress appropriately. Individual tickets are available up to two days ahead in person (at the Prudential Center or the New England Aquarium) or online; only group sales are available by phone. Summer tours often sell out by noon, so buy your tickets early. Vehicles depart from the Boylston side of the Prudential Center, though that will change in the future to a still undesignated site.

790 Boylston St.

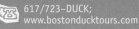 617/723-DUCK;
www.bostonducktours.com

 $23 ages 13 and up,
$20 students,
$13 youths 4–12, 25¢
children 3 and under

Apr–Nov, daily 9–1 hr before sunset,
every ½ hr

 All ages

on the Freedom Trail. Splashdown comes about a third of the way through. Once on water, children may even be invited to take the wheel (provided the water is calm). Narration is provided by lively "Con-DUCK-tors," who add a farcical flair to the adventure; on any given day, your driver could be the fearless Captain Courageous or the caped Captain Ridiculous. Outrageous getups aside, these captains are serious navigators with extensive knowledge of Boston history, and they have sea and land licenses that enable them to maneuver Boston both by river and road (the latter qualifying as a military operation all by itself).

Unlike some other local bus tours, the Duck trips are not stop-and-go excursions, meaning you won't be able to get out and amble around the various sights. Duck operators consider tours an overview of the city, and they encourage you to walk around it afterward. You might, then, consider the expedition the perfect Boston intro-DUCK-tion.

HEY, KIDS! The term "Duck" actually evolved from the WWII army abbreviation DUKW. "D" stood for the design year (1942); "U" for utility vehicle, "K" for front-wheel drive, and "W" for double rear axle (go figure these!). Is it any wonder that soldiers just called them Ducks?

BOSTON HARBOR CRUISES WHALE WATCHING

Northeasterners can be forgiven their skepticism about actually seeing whales on a whale watch. Most of us, after all, are unaccustomed to seeing any wild animal more exotic than a garbage-can-variety raccoon, much less Moby Dick tooling around free in our own backyard. But take a jaunt on Boston Harbor Cruises for a whale-watching excursion, and, amazingly, you may find exactly that: great, blubberish creatures lumbering around the waters of Massachusetts.

The trip takes three to four hours, so bring diversions and snacks and dress warmly any time of year, as the sea air brings a chill on deck (though cabins are comfy and climate controlled).Your destination is Stelwagon Bank, where school-bus-size creatures have made their feeding ground. Look for humpback, finback, and the diminutive (at least in whale terms) minke whales as well as the occasional dolphin. For the record, Moby Dick doesn't actually live here; he was a sperm whale, most of whom live in deeper waters. Awe-inspiring happenings during the roughly hour-long "show" may include spouting and

KEEP IN MIND Boats run rain or shine. Theoretically, they don't run in extremely choppy seas, but even so-called "not bad" days can be choppy enough to bring up lunch (trust me!). Tickets are nonrefundable, so if you're prone to seasickness, consider same-day booking so you'll have a sense of weather (though it may mean getting closed out on a nice day). At the very least, consider an OTC remedy. Other whale-watching expeditions: A.C. Cruise Line (290 Northern Ave., tel. 800/422–8419) and one through the New England Aquarium (Central Wharf, tel. 617/973–5206).

1 Long Wharf

 $29 ages 13 and up, $23 children 4–12

Apr–May Sa–Su 10:30, plus mid-Apr–May, M–F, 12:30 and late May, Sa–Su 2:30; June–Sept, M–F 9:30, 12:30, Sa–Su 8:30, 10:30, 12:30, 2:30, 5:30

617/227–4321 or 877/SEE–WHALE; www.bostonharborcruises.com

 5 and up

trumpeting (the deep-throated sound that accompanies spouting). Keep your eyes peeled for signs of other activities. The liftoff of birds (many of whom dog the whales for their "leftovers") could mean a whale is coming to the surface, and a fast dive might be the precursor to a breach, that coveted, albeit only occasional, dramatic leap in the air. Perhaps most amazing is proximity. If you're lucky, you just may get close enough to smell the whale's—ahem—aromatic breath. (The smell comes from bacteria in the whale spout.)

Whale-watching trips are suspended in late fall and winter, when the whales return to their warm Caribbean homes. Sightings are guaranteed; however, whether the adventure is a complete success is the luck of the draw. You can see dozens of whales or only one. In the event of a complete no-show, the cruise line will give you a ticket good for passage any time (no cash refunds, however).

HEY, KIDS! Did you know that whales eat the equivalent of 8,000 quarter-pounders a day just to keep their whale-ish figures? And though they all may look alike to you, humpback whales have very distinctive markings on the underside of the tails. Can you tell them apart?

EATS FOR KIDS Steps away from the dock, **Tia's** (200 Atlantic Ave., tel. 617/227–0828) specializes in all kinds of seafood—but no whale. Moms and dads can enjoy lobster or swordfish while kids get their own favorites: grilled cheese, chicken nuggets, and burgers. It's closed in winter. A few more steps down the street, **Joe's American Bar & Grill** (100 Atlantic Ave., tel. 617/367–8700) features an enormous menu of sandwiches, grills, and entrées.

BOSTON LIGHT

Anyone who thinks the Maytag repairman is the loneliest person on earth ought to talk to the guys on Little Brewster Island. These hearty souls staff the island's famous lighthouse—Coast Guard Light Station Boston, nicknamed Boston Light—the oldest lighthouse site in North America. The 220-year-old edifice is plopped 10 miles from downtown Boston, center stage in a small mound of rock and grass merely 600 feet long and 250 feet wide. Suffice it to say that a winter tour of duty here is a particularly long and lonely time.

But Little Brewster residents are feeling a bit less forlorn these days, now that they're entertaining guests. Back in 1999, the U.S. Coast Guard teamed up with the Island Alliance and the National Park Service to open up the small island for public tours. Oh sure, visitors could drop by before, but until recently, when public transportation was launched, getting here took either a private boat or a mighty strong pair of arms.

HEY, KIDS!
Look for the names of keepers carved into the island's rocks. No one's sure exactly how many there are. Suffice it to say, you'll find dozens dating all the way back from George Worthylake, Boston Light's original keeper. Worthylake drowned off the island in 1718.

KEEP IN MIND Purchase tickets by phone or at the Harbor Islands Store, U.S. Courthouse Arcade (1 Courthouse Way, Fan Pier). Reservations are highly recommended (past summers have sold out). Attached to the courthouse is a small interactive discovery center dedicated to the Boston Harbor Islands. If you've got your own boat, you're welcome to visit the island Friday–Sunday (donation requested). Children under 50" are not permitted to climb the tower, but many enjoy the island anyway.

Island Alliance, 408 Atlantic Ave.

617/223–8666;
www.bostonislands.com

 Sa–Su $25 ages 13 and up, $15 children 6–12; Th–F $4 more, but includes JFK Library

 Early June–mid-Oct, Th–Su 10 and 2

6 and up

There's little fanfare on this acre of land with six structures, but the lighthouse makes it worth the trip. Like much of Boston, the little building is steeped in history, from its construction in 1716 to its reconstruction after the British blew it to pieces in 1776.

You'll travel to the island on the 49-passenger *Hurricane*. Once there, you'll be invited to haul yourself up the lighthouse's 76 stairs, followed by two ladders, an unappealing prospect to some. The rewards are some stellar views of the harbor and surrounding islands. The island also has a small exhibit dedicated to the structure.

Boston Light's official role is for navigation and weather reporting, but the real function seems to be symbolic. Most of today's lighthouses are automated and have long been abandoned by official staff. In fact, Boston Light is the country's only beacon operated by active Coast Guard personnel, who keep watch over a wide swath of ocean and a little slice of history.

EATS FOR KIDS Walk toward Faneuil Hall and you'll find the **Green Dragon Tavern** (11 Marshall St., tel. 617/367–0055), a Colonial tavern with huge pub portions to fill you up after your outdoor adventure. Half-portions of Italian favorites at **L'Osteria Restaurant** (104 Salem St., tel. 617/723–7847), in the North End, will probably be plenty for kids. (If you're going for lunch, call ahead to make sure they're open.)

BOSTON TEA PARLOUR

Once upon a time, tea was the focal point of an afternoon. Each day at 4, ladies (and perhaps gentlemen) would drop what they were doing and settle down in the formal parlor for a sip of chamomile. Alas, the tradition has been watered down. Most people are too busy to spread the formal tablecloth at teatime, and it's hard to feel ladylike when you're slurping from a Styrofoam cup bought on the fly at the Dunkin' Donuts drive through.

Boston Tea Parlour owner Cynthia Alex has done her best to re-create those genteel days, however. She has dressed up her pretty little Victorian tea cottage in lace, crystal, and tapestry, even adorning her servers in traditional black and white. Dainty music plays while mothers, grandmothers, and daughters (we're not trying to be sexist here; it's just that the overwhelming sentiment is that tea is just not a "guy" thing) sip tea and nibble away at elegant Victorian tables surrounded by scads of pretty trinkets.

Light fare includes salads, scones, and sandwiches. Pint-size sippers will be delighted by

EATS FOR KIDS You'll probably get plenty to eat during your tea, but if you need more food, try out the delectable salads, breads, and sandwiches at the **Carriage House Cafe** (200 Great Rd., tel. 781/275–0095), open weekdays only. If all the gourmet stuff is wearing on your little tea-loving teetotaler, you can opt for the decidedly less formal **Victoria's Station** (128 Middlesex Tpke., Burlington, tel. 781/273–2230), about 2 miles away.

140 Great Rd. (I–95 Exit 31B), Bedford

 781/275-8768;
www.bostonteaparlour.com

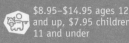 $8.95–$14.95 ages 12
and up, $7.95 children
11 and under

T–Su 11:30–4

6 and up

the "Little Princess" fare (for children 11 and under), which includes selections of heart-shape tea sandwiches (even peanut butter and chocolate—Nutella!) as well as fruit, dessert, and beverages. Decaffeinated fruit teas may appeal to the kids, but they can opt for fruit punch if they prefer.

Occasional events include visits by princesses, such as Cinderella, or perhaps even Mrs. Claus. The parlor hosts exceptional birthday parties (for children as young as 4), which include elegant private rooms, dress up, and crafts. Girls get to don a special boa during their stay, and all little guests get to take home a little bauble in the form of a piece of costume jewelry.

You don't have to get dressed up for the occasion—lots of moms and kids come in after school—but coming in chapeaus and lacy frocks definitely adds to the experience. Oh, and don't forget to lift your pinkies.

HEY, KIDS! The tea tradition supposedly began in Bedford—Bedford, England, that is. The legend goes that an impatient (and hungry!) duchess ordered her servants to tote up sweets and beverages to quell her hunger until dinner. The idea was a hit and was adopted by all ladies of status.

KEEP IN MIND Boston Tea Parlour isn't the only tea in town. Boston proper boasts two hallowed but much pricier tea halls: the new Ritz-Carlton (10 Avery St., tel. 617/574–7100) and the Four Seasons (200 Boylston St., tel. 617/338–4400). Plan to get dolled up. During December, the Four Seasons hosts a Teddy Bear Tea, in which bear-bringing children drink tea on the house; the bears (new bears, please) go to Children's Hospital. Refreshments include hot chocolate, apple juice, pastries, and teddy-shaped PB&Js.

BOSTON TEA PARTY SHIP

57

One night 2¼ centuries ago, a group of colonists descended on Boston Harbor dressed as Native Americans. Steaming about the injustice of "taxation without representation," they dunked hundreds of crates of unfairly taxed tea into the drink. As any student steeped in American history (not to mention punning) can tell you, that event started the brew that eventually boiled over into the American Revolution.

The *Brig Beaver II,* a full-scale, working replica of the smallest of the three ships assailed that December night in 1773, re-creates the protest. As part of ongoing shows, costumed colonists host a rousing and often heated town meeting, during which you can join in with traditional cries of "Fie" at the mention of unfair taxation and toss out suggestions for defying British rule. The course of action is put to a vote, but throwing the tea in the harbor always wins out over such creative ideas as stealing it and drinking it. Then it's off to the *Beaver II* to conduct the deed. Kids and adults alike take part in dumping the precious cargo, in reality, empty crates tethered to the ship by ropes.

HEY, KIDS!

How much tea went over the edge? More than 300 crates. Talk about a major download! The tea was worth roughly $33,000 then—probably over $1 million today—enough to hit King George squarely in his wallet. No wonder the event burned the Brits so much and caused them to act!

KEEP IN MIND

Though many historic attractions are good for kids studying the period, this particularly lively show often appeals to little ones as well. The ship's official season ends during the icy months of December, January, and February, but the attraction occasionally opens on balmy December days. The ship also conducts a reenactment on the Sunday before December 16, the Tea Party's actual anniversary. (You'll have to watch from the bridge, as the throngs of spectators would probably sink the boat.) The precise site of the event is marked by a plaque on a nearby commercial building, at 470 Atlantic Avenue.

 Congress St. Bridge

 617/269-7150;
www.bostonteapartyship.com

$8 ages 13 and
up, $7 students, $4
children 4–12

Mar–late May and mid-Sept–Nov, daily
9–5; late May–early Sept, daily 9–6

 All ages

Afterward, rabble-rousers are invited to tour the rest of the ship. Look for information about the original *Beaver,* which was sunk by a hurricane at the end of the 18th century, and about construction of the replica. Budding sailors can try their hand at the time-honored skill of knot tying. There's also an exhibit dedicated to the significance of tea itself. Though it's lost out to coffee over the years, tea was a Colonial favorite that appealed to both genders, enabling women to take part in political chats formerly reserved for men's smoking rooms. Such an onerous levy on something considered a staple was simply more than locals could abide.

In August 2001, a fire damaged the attraction and forced it to close temporarily. It's expected to reopen in spring 2004 or sooner.

EATS FOR KIDS It may have an ambiguous moniker, but the **No Name Restaurant** (17 Fish Pier St., tel. 617/338-7539) serves fresh seafood with character. Just a few steps from the ship, **Three Cheers** (290 Congress St., tel. 617/423-6166) has pub fare as well as a children's menu. About a five-minute walk to the other side of the Northern Avenue Bridge gets you to the **Barking Crab** (88 Sleeper St., tel. 617/426-2722), known for its reasonably priced fresh seafood. For kids, there are land-born entrées (such as burgers), too. The tasty crab-shack fare can be enjoyed inside or, in season, under the tent.

BOULDER MORTY'S

From the bottom, the edifices that make up Boulder Morty's don't seem so daunting. From the top—well, that's another story. Fortunately, you'll be so busy trying to figure out which hand or foot goes where (like a vertical game of Twister), you won't have time to notice how high you really are.

Though it seems every gym this side of Pike's Peak has spawned some sort of indoor rock climbing, Morty's (about 45 minutes from Boston) has given it a new dimension. Eight thousand square feet of climbing surfaces make the place a rarity in the northeast, a 40-station indoor mountain range spanning from a smooth novice climb to a jagged inverted peak.

Novice climbers first need to get the hang of belaying. The belayer holds the safety end of the rope and keeps the line taut enough to protect the climber from sudden drops. The $34 fee for the one-time introductory class, which includes equipment and climbing time, makes for a big initial investment, and once you've passed, you'll just pay for a

KEEP IN MIND Staff are always on hand for introductory classes, but the place has become so popular that advance reservations for belaying classes—at least the day before— are now a must. You can rent shoes for $6, but sneakers (preferably old ones—they might take a beating) are fine. A good rule for clothing: keep it loose, but not too loose, lest you hear your children chanting from below, "I see London, I see France..."

25 Otterson St. (2 mi off U.S. 3 Exit 5E), Nashua, NH

603/886-6789

Day pass $12, equipment $4–$6, introductory class $34

T 5–10, W–F 3–10, Sa 10–10, Su 11–7

4 and up

day pass and equipment. (Children under 12 don't need the class; they're not old enough to belay.)

Don't worry about getting your money's worth. Kids (and parents) often want to spend the day here—even in summer, since it's air-conditioned—and everyone goes home happily worn out. As for safety concerns, you'll have to sign the requisite waiver, but the protected environment, monitored by pros, feels very secure. The biggest risk seems to be to parents' egos, inevitably bruised when children grossly outperform their folks.

In between ascents, take five in the upstairs loft. The tables and chairs here make a perfect spot from which to marvel at some of the more experienced climbers. Crawling around the walls, they seem to defy gravity, like real-life Spidermen. "It's like a ballet," says one—a ballet 35 feet off the ground.

HEY, KIDS! Think you've mastered the art of indoor climbing? Think again. Morty's continually changes the configuration of climbing pegs to keep things interesting. For the greatest challenge, follow the black-and-orange-striped tags (tag colors indicate degree of difficulty).

EATS FOR KIDS Food from home can be stashed in the upstairs fridge while you climb, or you can order in from any number of restaurant menus that are kept at the front desk. If you'd rather eat out, you can find awesome deli sandwiches at the **Nashua Garden** (121 Main St., tel. 603/886–7363). The large menu (steaks, seafood, sandwiches, salads, kids' menu) at **Martha's Exchange** (185 Main St., tel. 603/883–8781) will please just about everyone, and there's even home-grown brews.

BUNKER HILL MONUMENT

Asking "Where was the Battle of Bunker Hill fought?" at first sounds like the equivalent of "What color was George Washington's white horse?" But the answer might surprise you. The infamous battle was actually fought on Breed's Hill (where the monument stands today), a slightly shorter mound of land about ½ mile south of the hill for which the battle is named. Why the discrepancy? It's anybody's guess. Some say the move was strategic (Breed's Hill is actually closer to Boston, making it an earlier point to head off the British); others chalk it up to plain old misnavigation born of a bad map and a dark night.

Either way, the feisty, decidedly unconventional Colonial army effectively surprised the British, constructing a rudimentary fort and digging in for the good fight. (For the record, the proper Brits considered hiding behind barriers to be entirely unsportsmanlike.) At sunrise on June 17, 1775, the British, who had been camped nearby, awoke to find the fort in place. They attacked, and, after three assaults in two hours, walked away with a victory. But it was not without a sacrifice, as they lost half of their 2,200 soldiers.

HEY, KIDS!

Colonial-era muskets weren't very dependable. It took 15–20 seconds to reload and shoot (a disadvantage when the enemy is advancing), and misfires were common, partly explaining why soldiers fired simultaneously. Besides, says one park ranger only half in jest, "If you only fire one, it's not very scary."

KEEP IN MIND A short walk away, a vivid telling of the battle can be found at the Charlestown Navy Yard Visitor Center (55 Constitution Rd., tel. 617/242–5601), formerly called the Bunker Hill Pavilion. Entitled "Whites of Their Eyes," (a phrase commonly—if erroneously—associated with Bunker Hill), the 18-minute presentation ($3.50 adults, $2 children 18 and under) operates April–December 9:30–4:30. Certain elements, such as the headless soldier, may be too ghoulish for some. June through August, ask about the schedule of musket-firing demonstrations. Children under 14 need to be accompanied up the stairs by an adult.

Monument Sq., Charlestown

 Free

 617/242–5641;
www.charlestown.ma.us/
monument.html

Daily 9–4:30; adjacent visitor center
daily 9–5

All ages

National Park Service rangers often give talks (roughly 15 minutes each) on the historic encounter and are always available to answer questions. Exhibited letters from British and Colonial soldiers recount in detail the events that took place that night. "Nothing could be more shocking than the carnage that followed the storming of this work," reads one. Dioramas accurately re-create the scene just as the British and Colonials saw it. Even those not enamored of American history will be impressed by the perfection of these miniatures.

The 220-foot obelisk, completed in 1842, is a marvel in and of itself. Granite had to be hauled in from Quincy and then stacked by hand. And the views from the top of the monument's 294 stairs will make you realize why the vantage point was so valuable.

EATS FOR KIDS The **Warren Tavern** (2 Pleasant St., tel. 617/ 241–8142), a restoration of a 1780 Colonial tavern, has just about every kind of burger you can think of, even one named for Paul Revere (inexplicably with Swiss cheese and mushrooms). You can also choose from seafood, sandwiches, and salads. The **Ninety-Nine Restaurant** (29/31 Austin St., tel. 617/ 242–8999) has the chain's huge selection of hamburgers, salads, grills, and other entrées.

BUTTERFLY PLACE

54

Question: What has 1,000 wings and flies? Answer: The Butterfly Place (or at least its collective residents). Founded in 1990, this private, family-owned business was born out of a penchant for airborne entomology (owner George Leslie started raising moths when he was 6 years old). Today this unusual facility houses roughly 500 butterflies representing about 50 different species, all fluttering around a 3,100-square-foot walk-through atrium.

Visits here start with a 15-minute film on the facts of lepidopteran life (from caterpillar to butterfly), which will elicit "ewws" or "wows" depending on your child's disposition. Then it's off to the atrium. Budding horticulturalists will no doubt be impressed by the varied plant life in the lovely indoor garden. The diversity represents what you might see in the tropics. Butterflies, like other notable beauties, are a pretty persnickety lot, each variety demanding its own set of perks. The monarch, for example, will only lay its eggs on the leaves of a milkweed plant.

EATS FOR KIDS Covered picnic benches provide a perfect spot to finish your nature expedition. For ribs, burgers, and chicken with an Aussie flare, try **Outback Steakhouse** (440 Middlesex Rd., tel. 978/649–8700). Aspiring firefighters may be distracted from eating by all the fire-fighting memorabilia at the **Firehouse Restaurant** (130 Middlesex Rd., tel. 978/649–4118). The huge menu includes burgers and steaks as well as homemade potpies and pot roast.

120 Tyngsboro Rd.
(U.S. 3 Exit 34), Westford

 978/392-0955; www.butterflyplace-ma.com/homeB.htm

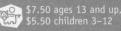 $7.50 ages 13 and up, $5.50 children 3–12

 Mar, daily 10–4; Apr–Columbus Day, daily 10–5; last atrium entry ½ hr before closing

All ages

Mr. Leslie breeds all the domestic varieties in-house; exotic inhabitants are recruited from spots like Florida and Costa Rica and hatched from pupae. (Lest you think about importing your own flock, think again; the pastime requires numerous permits.) Unhatched pupae are openly displayed, and if you're lucky, you might be able to watch a butterfly emerge. Or you might catch a praying mantis slowly preying on its dinner (a live wasp), a fascinating sight for those who can bear to look. At least one staff member is always on hand to answer questions and point out pertinent facts about the entomological world.

Do think carefully about how you dress for the occasion. Butterflies like their quarters warm—about 80°F. So even if it's cold outside, make sure to dress in layers to keep comfortable.

HEY, KIDS! To try to get a butterfly to land on you, stand very still. Wearing certain color clothes won't matter; the creatures can't tell them apart. Perfume is a bad idea, too; you won't fool them into thinking you're a flower. (Don't laugh; people have tried this!)

KEEP IN MIND The Butterfly Place welcomes all ages, but for the safety of these delicate creatures, children under 3 must be carried, kept in a stroller, or held by the hand. Visitors are free to gaze, gawk, and gander, but no grabbing. On the other hand, some precocious creatures might choose to temporarily perch on a fortunate visitor or two. Those who find such a prospect undelightful can simply give a gentle blow and they'll flutter off.

CASTLE ISLAND PARK

A stroll to this popular park, contrary to what you might think from the park's name, won't require a bathing suit, but you may want one while you're there. Castle Island isn't actually an island, though it was one when it was named (around the early 1600s). Since then, a causeway has joined this lovely crescent of land jutting out into the Boston Harbor—one of the farthest points you can venture to in the city without actually leaving dry land. That this faux island is today accessible on foot (as well as by car) makes it a haven for anyone out to enjoy the fresh air.

Roughly 2½ miles of promenade form a loop from Day Boulevard to Castle Island and back again. Pleasure Bay, the body of water at the center of the loop, is commonly referred to as Metropolitan Boston's largest swimming pool. You can access the water from any of the park's beaches. Paved paths around the bay accommodate different types of wheels—

KEEP IN MIND Although Castle Island's park is open year-round, Ft. Independence can only be accessed (via tours) weekends Memorial Day–Columbus Day. Tours are run by the Castle Island Association for the Metropolitan District Commission (tel. 617/727–5293). If you want to get spooked, take the Halloween Mystery Walk (call the MDC for info), an annual stroll through a ghoulishly decked-out fort. Castle Island is part of the larger Marine Park, which, in winter, includes the MDC's on-site skating rink.

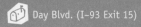 Day Blvd. (I–93 Exit 15)

617/268–5744;
www.state.ma.us/mdc/harbor.htm

 Free

Daily sunrise–sunset

All ages

stroller, roller, or bike. A playground and fishing pier are perfect outdoor diversions. If you'd prefer to tarry, picnic tables and park benches are ideal spots from which to sip soft drinks and watch the scenery (the views of the Boston skyline are magnificent). After all that drinking, you'll be happy to know that this castle is modern-facility equipped; bathrooms, however, are only open April–October.

If you're wondering, the island got its name from its military significance. Numerous forts were built here over the centuries, all informally known as the "Castle." The most modern—Ft. Independence, which dominates the island—was built in the mid-19th century. You can wander outside the fort on your own, but you'll need a guided tour to get inside. In addition to its military legacy, the immense stone structure is purported to have been the site of buried treasure and sea-serpent sightings.

EATS FOR KIDS To truly appreciate the splendor here, you'll want to bring your own eats and enjoy them in the out-of-doors. In season, **Sullivan's,** an on-site institution in these parts, provides the perfect accessories for the expedition: hot dogs, snacks, and sodas. Another institution, this one a year-round restaurant, is the family-owned **Farragut House** (149 P St., tel. 617/268–1212), a friendly place for fish, steak, ribs, and children's specialties.

CHARLES RIVER CANOE AND KAYAK

52

Most people associate the Charles with the wide stretch that separates Boston from Cambridge. However, the river actually begins in Hopkinton and extends 80 miles—much of it through rural communities—before reaching Boston city limits. Quiet expanses between Hopkinton and Waltham, the point after which the river becomes broad, straighter, and urban, are enormously peaceful, winding through marshes and past turn-of-the-20th-century estates. Though it's only a half-hour drive from the city to the spot where you rent and launch your craft in Newton, you'll feel as if you're on the other side of the world. Paddlers should keep a careful eye out for such resident wildlife as turtles—a big thrill for kids who've never seen one outside of a pet store tank. You'll have to look carefully, though, as the little green guys tend to blend in with the scenery. As for birds, you never know what you'll see, perhaps enormous great blue herons, ospreys, or Eastern orioles. Even muskrats call the area home.

KEEP IN MIND Peak hours are weekends and holidays between 1 and 3:30, so plan accordingly. Marshy territory is prime critter country, so don't forget the bug spray. Flip-flops or water shoes are a good idea, too. If you'd prefer to city gaze as you paddle, try the company's satellite office in Allston Brighton (tel. 617/462–2513). Look for its kiosk at the dock across the Elliott Bridge from Harvard Square. For canoeing on a lake, try the company's office in Natick, on Lake Cochituate (tel. 508/647–1700). In questionable weather, the latter two merit a call, as they sometimes close when it rains.

2401 Commonwealth Ave., Newton

 Std canoes $11 per hr; lg canoes, kayaks, pedal kayaks, rowboats $14 per hr; kids' kayaks $6 per hr

 Apr–Oct, M–F 10–5:30, Sa–Su 9–5:30; Nov–March, by appt

617/965–5110; www.ski-paddle.com/cano/canoe.htm

All ages

Rentals include mandatory life jackets. Hourly rates are optimal for short trips, but if you're planning a longer foray, consider the daily rates. Either way, keep an eye on time, since paddling one hour out means a second hour of paddling back, and that return trip can be a killer. You'll also want to consider your direction, as heading downstream on the way out means you'll be fighting the current (and perhaps the wind, which can dog you no matter which way you head) on the way home. On the other hand, traveling downstream enables you to dock near a playground for some added terra firma fun. From the perspective of scenery, however, the two directions are pretty similar.

HEY, KIDS! How many different kinds of turtles can you spot? The painted turtles are the little guys; the snapping turtles are the great big ones. Hint: Stay away from the big ones. They could bite. In fact, rangers say it's a good idea not to bother—or feed—any of the wildlife.

EATS FOR KIDS Sandwiches and bagels are on the menu at **Bruegger's Bagels** (739 Beacon St., tel. 617/630–9715). By contrast, **Blue Ribbon Barbecue** (1375 Washington St., West Newton, tel. 617/332–2583) dishes up authentic Southern fare. There are only 12 stools inside, but on a nice canoeing day, you can get takeout and enjoy it in the great outdoors.

CHILDREN'S MUSEUM OF BOSTON

Most kids would classify the term "science playground" as an oxymoron (that is, if they could define the term "oxymoron"). But that's not the case at this children's museum, where the seemingly mundane is turned into magic. A fixture on the Boston scene for more than 80 years, this much-loved institution first achieved fame as one of the original interactive utopias. Today's version, in a roomy building not far from the Financial District, more than lives up to its pedigree.

Three floors of activities can keep a family busy for hours. At the aforementioned Science Playground, kids (and their scientifically challenged parents) get a handle on some laws of nature by playing with soap bubbles or ball mazes. At the Giant's Desk, a longtime favorite, comparatively Lilliputian kids can take shelter in a behemoth pencil holder. For the other side of the size spectrum (i.e., miniatures), head to the extensive collection of dollhouses in the Hall of Toys. Today's globally oriented kids can play clerk or shopper in the Spanish-theme Supermercado, and children of the '60s can wax nostalgic in Grandparents

HEY, KIDS!
How different is it to live in Japan? Find out by poking your head into the authentic Japanese house on the museum's third floor (you can look but not enter). The tatami mats (for sleeping) will probably fascinate kids used to a traditional American bed.

EATS FOR KIDS A **McDonald's** (316 Congress St., tel. 617/482–1746) is "conveniently" attached to the museum. The bad news (beyond the effect on your cholesterol) is that the interior connection takes you through a gift shop. Wise parents take a short detour outside. On weekdays, enjoy salads or sandwiches at **Bethany's** (332 Congress St., tel. 617/423–5836); there are a few indoor tables, or eat outside. In late spring and summer, pick up snacks from the nearby **Milk Bottle,** aptly named for its shape. A short hike away, have your pick of eats at Faneuil Hall (see #38).

 300 Congress St.

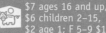 $7 ages 16 and up,
$6 children 2–15,
$2 age 1; F 5–9 $1

Sa–Th 10–5, F 10–9

617/426–8855 recording, 617/426–6500 voice; www.bostonkids.org

12 and under

House, whose period decor includes a Formica kitchen table and a black-and-white TV. Play vintage games in the living room, or wend your way upstairs into the attic, where old trunks are full of dress-up clothes that kids can actually put on.

Newer additions include Arthur's World, where, thanks to the magic of blue-screen technology, you can appear on a monitor alongside the world's most famous aardvark, and the self-explanatory Climbing the Walls.

School-age children go wild here, scaling the newfangled climbing sculpture, building (and, more importantly, knocking down) in the Construction Zone, and exploring the below-sea-level world in Under the Dock. But little ones need not be left out; tots (3 and under) have their own special haven in the Smith Family PlaySpace, a quiet, cozy spot with soft blocks, books, train sets, and crafts projects that's perfect on a weekday afternoon.

KEEP IN MIND Cost-conscious parents (and who isn't!) can take advantage of Friday's extended museum hours (5–9), when admission is $1 for all. The only down side is that you'll likely have to deal with larger-than-normal crowds. The museum's other down side at any time is its size. Count on running yourself a little ragged to keep up with your children here (though you'll at least be having fun) and relishing that much-deserved glass of wine (hot cocoa for the kids) when you get home.

COMMUNITY BOATING

I mages of Boston somehow don't seem complete without a picture of college crews sculling along the Charles River. The famed waterway, with the city as its backdrop, is a focal point of athletic pastimes. The banks teem with runners and bladers (*see* Dr. Paul Dudley White Bike Path), the water with oarsmen.

True, your kids may be too young to suit up with the Harvard crew team, but family sailing opportunities are available through this nonprofit organization. Wannabe Popeyes can sign up for a visitor pass (\$100) that nets unlimited sailing time and craft rental for you and three guests for two consecutive days, provided the helmsman can pass muster with the staff here first. Those without experience will have to plan ahead and sign up for the 45-day membership that includes lessons. The cost is still reasonable (\$75 per student), and once you've passed, you're in business to take the family along for the ride.

Less-experienced sailors might opt for a 14-foot Mercury boat, which holds up to four. More-

KEEP IN MIND Locals may prefer longer-term memberships, which—at \$125 for 75 consecutive days or a full year for \$175—are more economical than the two-day option. Once you've paid your membership, there is no additional rental fee for the boats. Lessons are held regularly throughout the week; call for a schedule. Experienced scullers can rent shells through Charles River Canoe and Kayak (*see* #52), which also rents canoes for the Charles River Basin and other locations. For a guided cruise down the Charles, try Charles River Boat Company (100 Cambridgeside Pl., tel. 617/621–3001).

21 David G. Mugar Way
(near Hatch Shell)

 $100 for 2 days of sailing, $125 for 75 days

 Apr–Oct, M–F 1–sunset,
Sa–Su 9–sunset

617/523–1038;
www.community-boating.org

5 and up; sailors 10 and up

experienced sailors can choose from sophisticated crafts that run up to about 22 feet. Boats launch from the Community Boating dock near the Longfellow Bridge and sail between it and the Massachusetts Avenue Bridge (the area commonly known as the basin). Kayaks and Windsurfers are available under the same membership; you'll have to prove worthy of these as well.

Daily boat rentals have no time limit; you just have to be back by sunset. On busy days, however, the staff may ask you to check in hourly to ensure that there's no waiting list (this may be a good time to bring along a cell phone so you don't have to keep returning to the dock). If you're unsure whether you qualify as "experienced," do yourself a favor and check your status out before sail day, thus avoiding disappointing wails of "But you pro-o-o-omised."

EATS FOR KIDS
The tasty Asian cuisine at the **King & I** (145 Charles St., tel. 617/227–3320) has made the restaurant a popular local haunt. American bistro fare at **Harvard Gardens** (316 Cambridge St., tel. 617/523–2727) includes comfort food as well as some more creative dishes.

HEY, KIDS! Want to be a sailor yourself? If you're age 10–18, you can join the summer Junior Program. From mid-June to late August, $1 buys all the lessons and watercraft rental you want for the season (certain hours apply). The program attracts 1,200 kids each year, but since attendance is staggered and there's a big fleet, getting a boat generally isn't a problem. To become a member, you must fill out an application, obtain parental permission, and show proof of your swimming capabilities.

COMMUNITY SOLAR SYSTEM TRAIL

T alk about a walking tour that's out of this world! Kids who turn their noses up at the Freedom Trail just might be lured into doing Boston on foot thanks to this novel tour. Best of all, in addition to walking, you'll be able to explore outer space by navigating some inner space (subway tunnels), too.

The tour is the creation of the folks at the Museum of Science. The sun, the hub of this solar system, is at the museum, and the nine planets (eight and a big rock, if you're persnickety about the designation of Pluto) are spread around the Boston area. Each bronze planet model is placed the appropriate relative distance from the sun. Your children's mission is to find each celestial body, make a rubbing in their official passport of the planet's symbol on the model (use pen, pencil, or crayon, as markers won't work), and bring home the passport with a mark for each.

HEY, KIDS!
The T is an old, but speedy, form of travel—in this case, interplanetary travel. Introduced in 1897, trains go up to 30 mph. Back then, rides cost a whopping 5¢; today it's up to $1 plus surcharge, a small price to pay to get to Pluto.

EATS FOR KIDS Stop after Mars at the **Cambridgeside Galleria** (100 Cambridgeside Pl., tel. 617/621–8666). In addition to a traditional food court, there's a **Cheesecake Factory** (tel. 617/252–3810), serving better-than-average chain fare and much-better-than-average desserts. There's also plenty of food at a **food court** at South Station (Jupiter). At **Full Moon** (344 Huron Ave., Cambridge, tel. 617/354–6699), after Saturn, you'll find not only mouthwatering Mediterranean specialties but also a play room. The kids' hot dog/fries combo comes with carrots, and there's m&c and green beans, too. Also see the Museum of Science.

Charles Hayden Planetarium at Museum of Science (*see* #24) and other area locations

 Passport free; museum $11 ages 12 and up, $8 children 3–11

 Museum July 4–Labor Day, F 9–9, Sa–Th 9–7; early Sept–July 3, F 9–9, Sa–Th 9–5; other planet sites vary

617/723-2500; www.mos.org/sln/wtu/css.html

8 and up

The first five planets are easily accessible by foot or T. In addition to the sun, Mercury and Venus are in the museum. Getting to Earth, at the Royal Sonesta Hotel, will take you about 10 minutes on foot. Mars is across the street at the Cambridgeside Galleria, and Jupiter is on the Red Line at South Station. Saturn, Uranus, and Neptune (in Cambridge, Jamaica Plain, and Saugus, respectively) are a little trickier. None requires a rocket to reach it, but you may need a combo of T and bus (or a car). Pluto is a straight shot from downtown, but it's way out in Newton (fittingly, the last stop on the Riverside Green Line), the equivalent of about 4.6 billion miles from the sun. Remember that you'll eventually need to get home, so though it may not be the most adventurous transportation, it's probably easier to just drive to Saugus.

When your family has reached every orb, mail the completed passport to the museum. You'll be rewarded with a certificate marking your accomplishment.

KEEP IN MIND Like any interplanetary navigator, you'll want to map out your voyage beforehand, perhaps opting for the most convenient, rather than strict numerical, planetary order. There's also no rule that says you have to visit all alien worlds in one day. And if you follow the tour in reverse, you'll end up at the Museum of Science and its Welcome to the Universe exhibit. Passports can be downloaded from the Internet (Welcome to the Universe section at mos.org) or picked up at the planetarium; either way, you'll get specific directions, parking information, and open hours for each site.

CURIOUS CREATURES KID'ZOO

You might call this place a petting zoo with attitude. No fuzzy barnyard here, this indoor tropical rain forest houses a jungle full of exotic critters, including baby alligators, snakes, iguanas, and tarantulas. It's a small place, perhaps too small for some older kids, but it offers a rare opportunity to get up close and personal with some mighty unusual specimens.

Creatures line every corner of the structure. Birds fly overhead, a macaw squawks, and large turtles swim around happily in open-air ponds. First-time visitors are often agog at the site of enormous iguanas crawling free on the rafters above their heads. Thankfully, the more intimidating species (tarantulas and alligators, for example) are kept in roomy enclosures. If you think your kids won't want to visit with the hairy spider (talk about a face only a mother could love), think again. Even kids who cry for help at the sight of an arachnid in their basement are fascinated by this oversize creepy crawly. Those who'd like to touch will need to talk to a staff member; the ultra-helpful folks can be identified by either their iguana T-shirts or the presence of a live snake or bird draped about their person.

KEEP IN MIND Animal-loving kids will want to spend a while here, so make sure you're comfortable. That means dress for the heat; in winter, layer sweaters over short sleeves and tank tops, and even sweatpants over shorts. And bring water, as there is absolutely nothing available. If your kids need to flex their fingers afterward, try Bonkers (535 Lowell St., tel. 978/535–8355), a whiz-bang arcade. The Kid'Zoo may open on weekends in the future; call ahead to check.

To be sure, your proximity to these unusual beasts (the animals, not the staff members) is pretty amazing, but equally impressive is the setting. Thick greenery and hanging vines effectively create a jungle look, and dim lights set the mood. Not content to have the place simply look like a jungle, owners Dean and Suzanne Kosch make it feel like a jungle, too—right down to the smell and the steamy heat. The place is a humid 85°F every day of the year, so you can kiss your good hair day good-bye.

Those concerned about animal rights can feel comfortable here. Kosch rescues all of the zoo's inhabitants from either inappropriate homes (would you believe someone actually kept an alligator as a pet?) or abandonment, and all are well-loved.

HEY, KIDS! Resident alligators live on a diet of rats. But how to keep a supply handy? Why, freeze them, of course! Just call it a ratsicle. The macaw lives on a much more civilized diet of fruit, seeds, and food pellets, but for occasional treats, he gets pizza and french fries.

EATS FOR KIDS You'll know you've reached the **Hilltop Steak House** (855 Broadway, Saugus, tel. 781/233–7700) when you spot the huge plastic cows on the front lawn. You'll have to drive about 15 minutes (toward Boston) to get here, but the kitschy place is a local institution for steaks. The animals on the walls talk at **Bugaboo Creek** (Northshore Mall, tel. 978/538–0100), where chain fare includes steaks, salads, and a children's menu.

DAVIS' FARMLAND

The phone number here spells "MOOO"; the fax spells "OINK." Need you ask how much Farmer Davis likes his livestock?

47

After more than 100 years of farming this acreage, the Davis family—father John and sons Larry and Doug—have found a new way to use their spread, namely reinventing it as a children's discovery farm. Sure, there's a little "moo, moo" here and an "oink, oink" there to listen to, but this is also an interactive adventure. The real treat is not just what your kids will see and hear, but what they'll get to do: feeding, milking, and some plain old-fashioned cuddling.

Farm residents include the usual suspects: your basic sheep, goats, pigs, and cows. (Most of the grown-ups are in pens, but some of the babies delight kids by wandering around their feet.) In addition, however, the Davis enterprise features some truly rare and unusual critters: Gloucester Old Spot pigs, long-haired Highland cattle, and Tamworth pigs, to

EATS FOR KIDS Corny? Sure. But the on-site **Herd Rock Calfe** is also pretty cute, serving up yummy burgers, dogs, and PB&Js. Thoughtful extras include baby food. For traditional Americana, try **Barbers Crossing North** (175 Leominster Rd., tel. 978/422–8438).

KEEP IN MIND The farm operates weather permitting, so call ahead if the day looks iffy. Farm activities, such as egg collecting (some of the chickens lay multicolor eggs) and cow and goat milking, occur at specified times throughout the day. Check for a schedule on the way in. Pony rides (extra fee) are also available. In summer, ask about special events featuring carnival-style performers. If you have older *and* younger children, you might want to buy a discounted combination pass for the farm and Davis' Mega Maze (*see* #46), across the street.

145 Redstone Hill Rd.
(off Rte. 62), Sterling

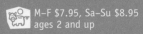 M–F $7.95, Sa–Su $8.95
ages 2 and up

 Mid-Apr–Labor Day, daily 9:30–4:30;
early Sept–Oct, Th–Su 9:30–4:30

978/422–6666;
www.davisfarmland.com

6 and under

name a few. Most folks are surprised to find farm animals on the endangered species list, but these rare creatures are. In fact, the main part of the Davis business is finding—and, in many cases, successfully breeding—such imperiled beasts, some of whose numbers have dwindled to mere hundreds.

That the discovery section is only a small portion of the 230-acre farm was part of a well-thought-out plan. Fathers themselves, the farmers understood the difficulty of trying to keep track of a wandering toddler or two. The discovery farm provides enough activities to entertain a young child in a space small enough (about 375 feet from center to edge) and well-enough designed (landings rise up as you walk outward, increasing visibility) to allow parents to stay in one place while seeing nearly the whole area. To view the rest of the spread, take a spin on one of the tractor-pulled hayrides or enjoy the fresh air in the sand, water, or climbing play areas.

HEY, KIDS! What is that funky-looking creature with the long, wooly hair and the donkey ears? That is a Patou—Pete the Patou, to be exact— a rare donkey from France. The odd-but-lovable animal used to be bred with a specific type of horse to create a kind of super mule, which was used to haul heavy items through the mountains. Alas, the popularity of motors made this offspring—and the Patous themselves—largely unnecessary. Pete is one of just a few of his kind left in the world.

DAVIS' MEGA MAZE

The sign says "Welcome," but it might just as well say "Get Lost!" That, after all, is the whole point of this confounding creation—to enter the sprawling tangle of corn plants and see how long it takes you to get out. Think it's a piece of cake? Think again.

Carved out of a 6-acre field of corn, the Davis maze has more than 3 miles of paths to navigate, with plants that tower as high as 10 feet and an elaborate sound system that keeps things lively. The average visitor takes 45 minutes–1½ hours to get to the other side. "The parents always joke on the way in about racing through and coming back later for the kids," muses Larry Davis, who, along with dad, John, and brother Doug, owns the farmland the maze is on. "But it's always the kids who make it out first."

Designed by renowned English maze maker Adrian Fisher, the Davis labyrinth takes on a new form each year. Previous designs have included dragons and Blackbeard (from above,

KEEP IN MIND Don't underestimate the maze's scope. It's absolutely not for people with claustrophobia or frail health. If you really must leave, find a staff member at any of the maze's bridges, and he or she will lead you out pronto. To avoid the need for an untimely exit, use the bathroom first; as the brochure says, "there's a portable toilet inside, but you'll have to find it." Also think ahead (and call) if there's been rain. Heavy downpours can create corn soup that closes the maze for a day or so. And the best plan with children 3 and under? Bring a backpack.

143 Redstone Hill Rd.
(off Rte. 62), Sterling

$9.95 ages 14 and up,
$7.95 children 4–13

 Mid-July–Labor Day, daily 10–5;
early Sept–Oct, Sa–Su 10–5

978/422–8888;
www.davisfarmland.com

4 and up

it really looked like a pirate). Inside, paths wind in every which direction. Fisher even adds a three-dimensional feature: bridges that can be crossed over and under.

Since the maze opened in 1998, some visitors have become very creative (or perhaps desperate), arriving equipped with cell phones and walkie-talkies. "It doesn't help," Davis says with a smile. Inside, staff members are on hand to give good-natured (and always on-the-level) prompts, such as "If I were you, I'd turn right." Don't despair if you do need some help; 90% of the guests here do. If you know you're going to have trouble, you can opt to carry a 10-foot flag; wave it around, and a staff member will appear at your side. Don't have a flag? Just look confused. The staff is instructed to offer help to those who appear to need it.

EATS FOR KIDS
The Davises keep a **grill** going with hot dogs and hamburgers and carry those all-important beverages. Despite its name, the **Sterling Ice Cream Bar** (167 Clinton Rd, tel. 978/422–7742) serves more than just the obvious; also look for seafood, sandwiches, and other fare at the attached restaurant.

HEY, KIDS! You'll probably be ready to go into the maze again even before mom and dad get out the first time (admission includes unlimited trips through), but it doesn't have to be the same adventure twice. It's possible to get to the end by crossing every bridge—or none at all. Set a different course for yourself, and see how much longer (or shorter) it takes.

DECORDOVA MUSEUM AND SCULPTURE PARK

45

M any an architect has made a reputation by fashioning a magnificent museum for art. At the DeCordova, Mother Nature has done a pretty splendid job on her own, carving out the perfect backdrop for art browsing alfresco.

Only 13 miles from the city, the DeCordova has a particularly bucolic setting—so peaceful, in fact, that Flint (or Sandy) Pond, behind the museum, was reportedly Thoreau's first choice for his return to simple living. (Unable to get the land, he ultimately chose Walden Pond instead.) Formerly the Julian DeCordova estate, the museum has put to good use both the grounds and the residential "castle," creating an ideal spot to introduce budding art appreciators to the world of sculpture and contemporary American art.

KEEP IN MIND The whole family is welcome. You can even bring dogs (on leashes) or bicycles. More extensive hiking trails are located behind the museum.

Roughly 80 works dot the Sculpture Park at any time, with creations ranging from abstract to fanciful. Pieces change frequently. Though such an assembly may look like a giant playground, the park is decidedly a no-climb zone. That's not to say that all you

HEY, KIDS! That Musical Fence sounds pretty dandy for a few minutes at a time. But what if you had to listen to it 'round the clock? The sculpture was originally commissioned for the city of Cambridge, but locals worried that though it was lovely, it would be a little too loud. As a result, the piece is on extended loan to the DeCordova.

51 Sandy Pond Rd.
(Trapelo Rd. Exit of I-95), Lincoln

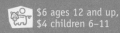 $6 ages 12 and up,
$4 children 6–11

 T–Su 11–5

781/259–8355; www.decordova.org

All ages

can do here is look, however. Some of the sculptures are open to touch—most notably the popular Musical Fence by Paul Matisse, an oversize xylophone that invites you to make music. And there is an increasing number of interactive offerings, including the aptly titled—and free—First Sunday program. Held the first Sunday of every month (for several hours in the afternoon), it uses such activities as scavenger hunts and crafts to help families explore exhibitions.

Those visiting on ordinary museum days find plenty to please, too. Family Activity Guides, located around the museum, contain ideas to help you explore on your own. Indoor galleries include the Dr. Kenneth Germeshausen Art ExperienCenter, an entertaining spot with virtual as well as paper-and-pencil art activities. Budding artistes should check out the extensive schedule of classes (extra fee). On the menu: photography, sculpture, yoga for artists, and just about anything else you can think of.

EATS FOR KIDS Picnickers are welcome, but you'll have to bring something to pack out your garbage, as there are no trash cans on the grounds. You can bring your own food or buy it at either the year-round, indoor **Café @ DeCordova** or the outdoor **Summer Café** (Memorial Day–Labor Day). Both are open Wednesday–Sunday 11–3 and serve sandwiches, soups, quiches, desserts, and drinks. Also see restaurants under Walden Pond.

DISCOVERY MUSEUMS

44

It's not hard to figure out what parents like about this homespun spot north of Boston. You certainly could find showier places, but for pure indoor exploration value, this duo is worth gold.

Two buildings make for one giant discovery. Up front, a cozy renovated Victorian house shelters the Children's Discovery Museum, for younger kids. Ten themed rooms span three floors, all filled with toys to fuel the imagination. The smell of soap bubbles permeates the Water Discovery room, where kids can dive into buckets of water for bubble play (in the figurative sense, thank you). Wall-size chalkboards let mural artists go to town; they can also make sidewalk masterpieces on the driveway outside. Lush (painted-on) greenery and props in the Safari and Jungle rooms are perfect places to go wild. Bessie's Play Diner has old-style booths, counter, stools, and plenty of cooking utensils and "food," and in this kitchen, parents get to be waited on for a change.

KEEP IN MIND Staff at the Children's Discovery Museum strive to keep it from getting too cozy, meaning at busy times, you may have to wait to get in. Entry is staggered through the use of numbers (like at the deli), but here you can grab a number, leave, and come back. Don't fret if your number is called while you're gone; you'll still be admitted on the spot. The museums seem to have gotten particularly popular of late, so come early. Entry to the larger Science Discovery Museum is usually not a problem. To spot the place, look for the giant dinosaur outside.

177 Main St. (near Rte. 2), Acton

978/264-4201;
www.ultranet.com/~discover

 $7 1 museum,
$10 both museums
ages 1 and up

 Mid-June–early Oct, T–Su 9–4:30; rest of yr,
children's T, F 1–4:30, W–Th, Sa–Su 9–4:30;
science T, Th–F 1–4:30, W 1–6, Sa–Su 9–4:30

Children's museum 1–6,
science museum 6–12

Out back, the newer Science Discovery Museum is designed for schoolkids. Two stories house dozens of science experiments to push, pull, stomp, and roll. Traditional wares include magnet play, pendulums, and recyclable crafts, to name only three, or see if you can manipulate a Ping-Pong ball using just the airflow from a blow dryer. Some exhibits are purely visual: the enormous box of bread tags (those little plastic things that hold the bread bag closed) gives a quantitative handle on the concept of "1 million" (it's astounding). Activities aside, the science center's greatest achievement is layout; there's enough to keep kids plenty busy without rendering them overwhelmed.

Dozens of books accompany activities at both museums, meaning tots can curl up with a story, and older kids can look up further information about the various sciences if their interest is piqued.

HEY, KIDS! Don't overlook those giant satellite dishes outside. They're not for TV reception but instead can help you discover the strange ways that sound travels. Stand at one while a friend stands at the other. Now take turns whispering. How well can you hear each other?

EATS FOR KIDS If your kids feel like making a new discovery in the food department, take them for some tasty Thai food up the street at **Benjarong Restaurant** (214 Main St., tel. 978/635–9580). If you must go for more standard fare, there's a **Friendly's** (387 Massachusetts Ave., tel. 978/263–0530) less than a mile away.

DREAMS OF FREEDOM MUSEUM

T hough New England is famous for early immigration (remember Plymouth Rock?), most people think of New York's Ellis Island when pondering latter-day arrivals. So it might come as a surprise that Boston is number two as a port of entry for immigrants, having welcomed more than 100,000 newcomers per year to American soil in the early 20th century.

Such is the hook of this relatively new addition to the Boston museum trail. Located on Benjamin Franklin's birth site (Franklin, for the record, was born here, but his father came from England), the 10,000-square-foot facility explores the path of immigrants—everything from how they came to what they brought. Though Old Ben's house burned down long ago, the site provides a historic spot to launch the adventure.

Far from giving just a flat retelling of old stories, the museum employs what the National Institute of Boston (the social services agency behind the museum) likes to refer to

HEY, KIDS!
The Golden Stairs aren't from a fairy tale; they're real, once leading from the old (and long defunct) East Boston immigration station. Why they're called "golden" is the million-dollar question. One theory has it that the stairs' handrails shone gold in the afternoon sun.

EATS FOR KIDS Discover English culinary roots at the **Elephant & Castle** (161 Devonshire St., tel. 617/350–9977), a British pub featuring all the staples—shepherd's pie, bangers and mash, and fish-and-chips—as well as a full range of English beers for mom and dad. For more international flair, head to **Empire Garden** (690–698 Washington St., tel. 617/482–8898), in nearby Chinatown, for some amazing dim sum.

1 Milk St.

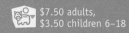 $7.50 adults,
$3.50 children 6–18

 Daily 10–6

617/338–6022;
www.dreamsoffreedom.org

10 and up

as "Disney-esque" touches, with high-tech wizardry designed to attract the attention of today's high-tech generation. What that means is that you can expect to be immersed: a ship deck pitches, a gangplank moves, and walls whisper. Holographic "hosts" guide you through—there's even a holo-video Ben Franklin who plays master of ceremonies.

Artifacts, newspaper clippings, and photographs add to the picture, and you can wrap up your visit with a stint in a video booth, where you can add your own family story to the melting pot. Just record your name, digital image, and a three-minute narrative. Though the museum is designed for elementary schoolkids, there are enough bells and whistles to keep younger children busy, too. Want more exploration? Pick up a map detailing the Immigrant Trail, which starts with the Irish Famine Memorial right outside the museum's door. If the adventure has stirred your curiosity about genealogy, check with staff members about how to use the Internet to research your family tree.

KEEP IN MIND Consider adding to your experience with a guided walking tour of the Immigrant Trail, run by Historical Entertainments (tel. 781/648–0628) throughout the year. Dedicated actor/guides immerse themselves in characters such as Ben Franklin, Abigail Adams, or a fictional immigrant, complete with appropriate garb.

DR. PAUL DUDLEY WHITE BIKE PATH

One of the best things about Boston is the Charles River. The waterway is a focal point of boating activity, from the sailboats that dot the horizon in the summer to the Head of the Charles regatta in fall, which literally fills the basin with college crew teams. Devout landlubbers need not feel left out, however; there are plenty of vantage points to enjoy the goings-on. Planners and landscape architects obviously thought carefully about how to maximize use of this picturesque river, installing miles of surrounding paved paths for those on foot, skates, and bicycle.

Approximately 18 miles of path—named for a renowned local cardiologist—stretch from Galen Street in Watertown Square, to the dam at Science Park. Sprinkled along the way are lots of park benches, fields, and public pools, as well as well-equipped playgrounds.

The best-known paths are those closest to Boston. Certainly among the busiest (sometimes perilously so), the trails travel both the Cambridge and Boston sides of the river, but you'll

KEEP IN MIND Come to Memorial Drive around April–October, when a section near Harvard Square is closed to cars 9–dusk. Beware: it's very busy. In May the Watertown Dam (above Galen Street) has a spectacular fish run (scads of herring come to breed); there's also a public swimming pool and spray pool. Another good ride, the 10½-mile Minuteman Commuter Rail, mirrors Paul Revere's ride, but it's also very busy. In-line skaters can also try the outdoor Reservation Road Skateboard Park (140 Reservation Rd., Hyde Park, tel. 617/635–4505) or Skater Island (see #9), indoors.

Both sides of Charles River, between Science Park and Galen St., Watertown Sq.

 Free

Daily sunrise–sunset

617/727-5114;
www.state.ma.us/mdc/images/bike2.gif

 All ages

be wise to stick to the latter, as they are generally set back a bit from the road. The Hatch Shell is a nice place for a rest (look for events during warmer months). You might also detour across the Larz Anderson Bridge to appreciate the funkiness of Harvard Square. But beware of traffic (bike, blade, and car) on the paths as well as at teeming crosswalks. Look for the alternative underpasses at the Elliott Bridge.

Those with young children are probably better off hitting the road farther west. At Artesani Park (off Soldier's Field Road in Brighton), you'll find great places to play (with new playground equipment) and to stash your car. Farther upriver, a 2-mile loop west from Watertown Square and back again (travel between Galen and Bridge streets) is short on traffic and long on scenery. Taken together, the stretch from Artesani to Watertown plus the loop is about 6 miles, but it's all relatively flat—and mostly set away from the road—so even kids can travel at a good clip.

EATS FOR KIDS
Harvard Square's **Au Bon Pain** (1360 Massachusetts Ave., Cambridge, tel. 617/661–8738) has good chain fare and great people-watching, and **Brew Moon Restaurant & Microbrewery** (50 Church St., Cambridge, tel. 617/499–2739) has hearty pub fare. For kebabs with Greek flair, try **Demo's** (84 Mt. Auburn St., Watertown, tel. 781/924–9660).

GETTING THERE If you're planning on taking a train to your starting point (say, to Harvard Square) you'll need a bike permit. Bikes are allowed on the Blue, Red, and Orange lines as well as on the commuter rail, but not on the Green Line. There are a whole list of dos and don'ts, so call the MBTA (tel. 617/222–3200). If you're going to Watertown, you'll have to drive, as bikes are not permitted on buses. Driving to the Charles? Look for parking lots on Soldiers Field Road across from the Harvard Stadium.

DRUMLIN FARM

J ust a few minutes from the bustle of Boston, this sizable working farm provides a bucolic respite for kids in the big city. More than 200 acres of farmland get worked throughout the year, and all the standard barnyard creatures are here, accompanied by their respective sound effects.

The heart of the operation, the Farm Core, is a short walk from the entrance. This is where you'll find the classic red barn as well as a chicken coop and pigsty. The cast of livestock includes milking cows, goats, draft horses, great big pigs that look very happy in dirt, and a couple of noisy roosters roaming around free. Watch out for impromptu vocal performances by these guys! Though Drumlin is not a petting zoo, it offers frequent demonstrations (e.g., cow milking) that get you up close to some of the animals. On occasion, you can even enter the chicken room and gather eggs. (Plan on purchasing the eggs you collect.)

HEY, KIDS!
How does a chicken chew without teeth? The secret is in the feed. Chicken chow includes hard material made of ground oyster shells. The bits of grit help grind the food in the birds' gizzard, part of their digestive tract.

KEEP IN MIND Baby-animal lovers will want to come in spring, when mamas-to-be are ready to have their little ones. Chicks generally start arriving around the end of March or beginning of April; lambs arrive from late February to early March. Public programs, including cow milking and animal education, are held daily in season, weekends only from November to March. Hayrides operate daily April–November (extra charge). Call for recorded information about the day's activities.

208 S. Great Rd.
(Rte. 117, near Rte. 126), Lincoln

 $6 ages 13 and up,
$4 children 3–12

 Mar–Oct, T–Su 9–5; Nov–Feb,
T–Su 9–4

 781/259–9807;
www.massaudubon.org/Nature_Con-
nection/Sanctuaries/Drumlin_Farm

12 and under

Beyond the central farm, five trails lead to remote fields and pastures. Keep your eyes open; you may spot a fox, coyote, rabbit, or weasel—as well as some rescued animals and birds housed in habitats near the Farm Core. Walk to the top of the drumlin, the glacial deposit the farm is named for, and be rewarded with some great views. On a clear day, you can see all the way to Mt. Wackiest. Stroller-pushers will have to stick to the main paved roads, except in summer, when the dirt paths tend to dry out enough for wheels to pass.

One word of warning: the animals' cute and cuddly appearances mask some harsh realities of farming, namely meat production. The freezer at the entrance advertising farm-fresh pork and beef may engender questions. Parents of young children should be prepared for some discussion.

EATS FOR KIDS Open March–December, **Dairy Joy** (331 North Ave., Weston, tel. 781/894–7144) is one of those much-loved neighborhood spots where you can enjoy sandwiches, burgers, and ice cream alfresco. Year-round, you can sit inside and dine on Italian food at **Racine's** (Rte. 117, Concord, tel. 978/371–3280).

ECOTARIUM

You have to hand it to the folks who named the EcoTarium (formerly called the New England Science Center). It may be a made-up word (then again, "on-line" wasn't in the dictionary once), but the bon mot perfectly describes this interactive science exploratory dedicated entirely to studying the environment. On 60 acres of wooded land, the EcoTarium uses all of its wares to convey its message. Indoor exhibits explain about our environment; outdoor exhibits actually let you explore it.

Half the adventures take place in the three-story exhibit hall. Use all of your senses to investigate the ecosystem that is New England in Look, Touch, and Feel. In the MicroDiner, microscopes reveal what might be taking up residence in pond water or your kitchen cabinets (you'll never look at expired grocery items the same way again).

What keeps the EcoTarium from being just another science center is its resident wildlife. Working as a rescue facility, the institution houses dozens of animals—from bald eagles

KEEP IN MIND Major renovations have spiffed up the 175-year-old place, so if you haven't visited in a while, expect improvements. Changing programs include story times, crafts, and vacation-week activities. Those ages 7 and up can take a guided tour of the Tree Canopy Walkway, which takes you 40 feet up into the trees, just like field researchers. You'll have to learn the ropes first—literally—as participants are secured by ropes. Call and ask about dates, times, and fees. Another popular feature is the 15-minute ride on the narrow-gauge Explorer Express Train (extra charge).

222 Harrington Way (Massachusetts Tpke. Exit 11), Worcester

 $7 ages 17 and up, $5 children 3–16

T–Sa 10–5, Su 12–5

508/929–2700; www.ecotarium.org

3–12

to a polar bear—all of whom have been injured or abandoned. (Sadly, Ursa Minor, the facility's second polar bear, died recently at age 35—a ripe old age for a polar bear in captivity.) "All of our animals have a story," says a staff member, and because of injury or socialization issues, all will reside here permanently. You can visit with small critters—turtles, a scarlet macaw, and an iguana, among others—in the exhibit hall and see golden lion tamarin monkeys and a boa constrictor in the new Endangered Species Building. More animals are housed outside along the two self-guided nature trails: the Timescape Trail and the Lower Loop Trail. When you've had enough active investigation, take a seat at the pavilion on the serene pond and revel in watching the world around you.

And if our world is too confining, explore the universe beyond by attending a show at the on-site planetarium or one of the occasional night-sky watches that uses the EcoTarium's high-powered telescopes (extra charge for both).

EATS FOR KIDS
Indoor vending machines provide all-important snacks. In warm weather, the outdoor **grill** sells hamburgers, hot dogs, and the like. For a bigger selection, take Route 9 to **Vinny Testa's** (7–11 Boston Tpke., Shrewsbury, tel. 508/755–0900) or to any of dozens of other eateries on the same route.

HEY, KIDS! What's a boa constrictor's favorite dish? Live mouse. That may seem impossible given their seemingly tiny mouths, but they manage. In order to open wide, the slithery guys have mastered the art of dislocating their bottom jaw, enabling them to consume their prey whole. If you're "lucky" (luck being a relative thing), you might get to observe the resident boa constrictor having dinner. Prospective snake owners, take note: the huge creature here started out as someone's small pet.

EDAVILLE RAILROAD

Ellis Atwood probably never expected his Christmas tradition to get quite this big. A cranberry farmer, Atwood used his narrow-gauge railroad—originally purchased to transport berries—as a sort of living holiday card, taking friends for scenic rides around his brightly Christmas-lit farm. Word got out about the excursions, and lo and behold, a business was born.

Christmas rail rides stayed a tradition at the Atwood farm until 1991, when the proprietors shut them down (Atwood had since died). Nine years later, new owners came on board, restoring the sheen of the old engines and relaunching them into service.

Though Atwood's original vision was for Christmas excursions only, today you can board the trains about half of the year. (It's even hoped that summer operations will begin by Memorial Day in the future.) Scenic trips around the 1,800-acre property (a roughly

EATS FOR KIDS The on-site **Freight House Café** has all the essentials (sandwiches, salads, snacks). In summer and fall, look for barbecue chicken at Edaville's **Choo Choo Chicken Barbecue;** at Christmas, warm cider and other treats. **Cornerstone's** (96 N. Main St., tel. 508/866–2665) is known for its bar and grill fare.

KEEP IN MIND If you want to learn more about the business of cranberries, head over to Ocean Spray Cranberry World (158 Water St., Plymouth, tel. 508/747–2350). The center details the history of the cranberry from Native American days until now and offers a tasting of 10 different types of juices. Cranberry World is open daily, roughly mid-May through November; admission is free. Labor Day through October, the Carver area is also home to the medieval antics of King Richard's Faire (Rte. 58, tel. 508/866–5391).

7 Eda Ave. (Rte. 58, off I–495), Carver

 July–Aug, F–Su 11–6; Sept–mid-Oct, Sa–Su 10–5; early Nov–early Jan, M–Th 4–9, F 4–10, Sa 2–10, Su 2–9

 $15 ages 3 and up; Christmas and special events $19.50 and up

877/EDAVILLE recording, 508/866-8190 voice; www.edaville.com

All ages

5½-mile circuit) take about 30 minutes, with passengers chugging along in vintage box cars behind turn-of-the-20th-century engines. The current crop of trains relies mostly on diesel power, but there is one vintage steam engine. Trains are stationed at Edaville's Victorian-style village, where a railroad theme park also contains eight children's rides, including an antique carousel, an antique fire truck offering 10- to 15-minute rides, and trains and farm equipment to climb on. A $5 million rehab, begun by the new owners, promises to polish the place to a nostalgic glow.

Still, the highlight of a visit here is unquestionably the train ride. Autumn riders can witness the cranberry harvest—watching as the flooded bogs become crimson with floating berries. The Christmas tradition features elaborate lights—more than 5 million of them—as well as a visit from that jolly old fellow from the north.

HEY, KIDS! There was no Presidents' Day back in the 17th century (not surprising, since there was no president), not to mention no Veterans', Memorial, and Martin Luther King, Jr., days, so children had to find other ways to get out of school. Fortunately, there were cranberries. Back in those days, the little red fruit was so important that at harvest time, schoolhouses (and businesses) were shut down so that everyone could help.

FANEUIL HALL

Boston-area newcomers are often confounded by local monikers that don't sound like they're spelled. Hence tourists routinely ask for Fan-wheel or Fan-oil Hall (it's really Fan-yuhl or Fan-uhl). Equally confusing is that Faneuil Hall does not refer to the nearby retail area with which it's often confused—Quincy (pronounced Quin-zy) Market—but rather just to the historic Great Hall, the nation's first public town meeting house.

Built in 1742 by Peter Faneuil, the hall acquired the nickname "Cradle of Liberty" after playing host to numerous meetings during which Colonists (verbally) blasted the British. Organizers of the Boston Tea Party originally met here, but the gathering got so large that it had to reconvene in the Old South Meeting House. The hall's modern-day legacy includes the launch of presidential candidacies for John F. Kennedy and Michael Dukakis.

Today Faneuil Hall retains its status as a multipurpose meet-and-greet spot, but most modern gatherers come sporting an ice cream cone (Steve's, in Quincy Market, is an absolute must!)

KEEP IN MIND With roughly 40 acts, there's bound to be performers here on any summer day. Special events take place for St. Patrick's Day and during the winter holidays, too. You can get a schedule of events and street performers by calling the Faneuil Hall Events Line (tel. 617/523–1300). Twenty-minute horse-and-carriage tours (for hire at North and Clinton streets) are another old-fashioned, albeit pricey ($35), diversion. On Congress Street, look for the graceful Holocaust memorial, and a few blocks in the other direction, let kids run off steam at the waterside Christopher Columbus Park.

 0 Faneuil Hall Sq.

 Free

617/523–1300;
www.faneuilhallmarketplace.com

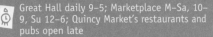 Great Hall daily 9–5; Marketplace M–Sa, 10–9, Su 12–6; Quincy Market's restaurants and pubs open late

All ages

or a latte rather than an agenda. The Great Hall itself is one of the few historic buildings that you can still enter free of charge, although it may be closed during special events. Daily 15-minute talks by park rangers (every half hour) detail the building's history, and revolutionary weaponry is on display in the Museum of the Ancient and Honorable Artillery Company, on the fourth floor.

For those too young to appreciate the historic majesty, the area also boasts daily street performances during fair-weather months, roughly March–October. The jugglers, storytellers, musicians, and other entertainers here are some of the country's best and are often hilarious. Sadly (for parents' wallets, anyway), the historic landmark is surrounded by Quincy Market's shrine to retail. Those who must have a new Boston souvenir will find the place brimming with knickknacks as well as more high-end merchandise—a far cry from what Sam Adams envisioned.

HEY, KIDS! Check out the grasshopper weather vane atop the Great Hall. The oversize *locustidae* (the insect family that includes the grasshopper) has symbolized the port of Boston since the 1600s. Of many legends surrounding it, one has it that it was a wealthy London merchant's good luck charm and was borrowed by Faneuil.

EATS FOR KIDS The question isn't where to eat here, but how much. Slightly surly service is part of the charm at **Durgin Park** (340 Faneuil Hall Marketplace, tel. 617/227–2038). Enormous portions of steak, seafood, and other fare are often accompanied by long waits. Inside the Quincy Market building, take your pick of a couple dozen vendors, from **Brown Derby Deli** (tel. 617/742–3028) and the Greek **Mykonos Fair** (tel. 617/742–8349) to tons of delicious bake shops.

FENWAY PARK TOUR

Y ou can't grow up in Boston without knowing about the Green Monster, a fixture in these parts since 1912. Unlike most ogres, however, this one doesn't torment children in pajamas, but rather grown men in pinstripe pants.

The monster, of course, is not a "who" but a "what." Towering 37 feet, the enormous green left-field wall is compensation for Fenway Park's diminutive size (only 310 feet from home plate to left). To get up close to the monster, your kids will either have to play outfield for a Major League ball club (provided Fenway is still standing then) or take one of the hourly 50-minute guided tours, which tell about Red Sox history and provide access to key spots within this fabled landmark.

The tour reveals all sorts of Fenway lore: about the greats who've played here, Babe Ruth and Ted Williams included; that the park was named for its neighborhood (the Fens),

HEY, KIDS!

How's your knowledge of Morse code? The dots and dashes on the Big Green Monster actually spell something. Can you figure out what it is? (Guides give the answer near the end of the tour.)

EATS FOR KIDS If you're not planning to stay for a game and chow down on lots of concession food, head over to **Pizzeria Uno** (1 Brookline Ave., tel. 617/262–4911), which has the chain's exceptional pizza plus some tasty Italian salads and pastas. If you're up for an active meal, **Jillian's** (145 Ipswich St., tel. 617/437–0300) is a local institution offering pub grub and a building full of arcade games.

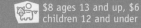

not the other way around; about the 1920 trade of Babe Ruth to the Yankees, resulting in the infamous "curse of the Bambino"; and the reason for the net above the monster, to protect pedestrians on Lansdown Street.

Sights on the tour include the press level (command central), where the organ music and public addresses originate; the premium 600-Club seats; and a private luxury box, available only on some tours. But the moment of moments comes when you step down on field level. You won't be able to round the bases, but you can walk on the warning track, getting close enough to the Green Monster to "hug it, kiss it, and throw yourself against it," as one guide put it. (You're simply asked not to leave any dirty fingerprints—or tears.) And there's nothing like the vantage point you get from a seat in the Red Sox dugout. The only thing that's missing is one of those greasy vendor sausages. For that, you'll have to come to a game and sit in the stands.

KEEP IN MIND Reservations are only taken for groups of 15 or more; otherwise, it's first come, first serve. Tickets are sold for the same day, in person only, and it's wise to buy early in the day (the box office opens at 8:45) to avoid sellouts. It's also wise to call ahead on tour day to confirm availability, as special events can alter the schedule or restrict field access. Features of the tour are subject to change.

FRANKLIN PARK ZOO

Along the Rodney Dangerfield of zoos—for years locals named it the country's worst—this zoo has had something of a renaissance. True, it's seen some challenges, but those who haven't visited in a while will be happily surprised.

Lowland gorillas are star residents of this urban zoo, which numbers several hundred creatures, among them zebras, leopards, exotic birds (even a couple of peacocks strutting around free), and slithery reptiles. The aforementioned gorillas, including a scene-stealing youngster, live in the Tropical Forest, home to other primates as well. Large glassed-in areas were designed to give humans the best view, but those expressive faces staring back from the other side might make you wonder who's watching whom. Outside the Tropical Forest, African wild dogs are among the zoo's newer additions.

Elsewhere, Chris and Cliff—two African lions—live happily in their Kalahari Kingdom, and a couple of long-necked neighbors dwell in the Giraffe Savannah. Zookeepers are adding some

KEEP IN MIND The good news about visiting in winter is that you'll see fewer people and perhaps a discount. The bad news is that you won't see the giraffes (they stay in their barn November–March except for very warm days) or the butterflies. Zoo New England, the nonprofit that operates this zoo, also runs the Stone Zoo (Pond St., Stoneham, tel. 781/438–5100), which has undertaken some much-needed renovation. Diminutive Capron Park (201 County St., Attleboro, tel. 508/222–3047) has a few animals and some playground equipment, good for smaller children, and Rhode Island has the outstanding Roger Williams Park Zoo (1000 Elmwood Ave., Providence, tel. 401/785–3510).

panache by creating natural habitats (an image hampered by the sight of apartment buildings beyond the endangered Bactrian camel habitat). The lion home, though on the small side, is indeed reminiscent of terrain the big cats might inhabit in Africa. Lots of large-pane windows give clear views of the felines, and props, including bleached animal bones and a Jeep wedged halfway inside the habitat, are effective scene setters. (To feel like you're on safari, look through the Jeep's windshield.) Wallabies and kangaroos inhabit the Australian Outback Trail, and you'll find zebras, ostriches, and ibex in the Bongo Congo. The seasonal (late May through September) Butterfly Landing requires an extra $1 fee.

Acres of wide, flat paths make the zoo a particular favorite for families with young children who need to run. At the sizable Franklin Farm and its "contact corral," you'll find the expected (goat, sheep, etc.) as well as some unexpected barn dwellers, such as owls and snakes.

HEY, KIDS! Snow leopards can leap 15 to 20 feet—straight up—in a single bound. That's about equivalent to the height of a 1½- to 2-story building. Take that, Superman.

EATS FOR KIDS The number of dining options depends on the season. During warm weather, the **Kalahari Kitchen** offers fresh pizza, snacks, and drinks, whereas the **Outback Barbecue** has grilled chicken and burgers. The **Giddy-Up Grill,** the only zoo eatery open year-round, features burgers, hot dogs, chicken tenders, and snacks as well as indoor and outdoor seating. Also see restaurants under the Blue Hills Trailside Museum and Reservation.

FREEDOM TRAIL

35

Kids who've grown up on video games and search engines may consider historic sightseeing the entertainment equivalent of brussels sprouts. But get to walking the Freedom Trail, and everybody has a good time.

This historic trail, created in 1958, links some of the area's most famous landmarks—living-history style. Follow the red-lined path to the home of Paul Revere, where you can try on Colonial garb; the Old North Church (*see #21*), where you can walk up to the loft where the famed lanterns were hung; and the Old South Meeting House, where defiant patriots conceived the idea for the Boston Tea Party. Most of the sites are free; others charge a nominal fee.

Experts recommend starting at Boston Common (*see #62*). From here, the 2½-mile trail wends through Beacon Hill, downtown, and the North End before concluding in

EATS FOR KIDS Pause on your historical journey at the equally historical **Union Oyster House** (41 Union St., tel. 617/227–2750), America's oldest restaurant (1826). The tasty food includes seafood and grills. For a modern experience, hop the T to the **Hard Rock Cafe** (131 Clarendon St., tel. 617/424–7625).

KEEP IN MIND Abbreviated (90-minute) seasonal tours of "the heart of the freedom trail" are offered by both the National Park Service and Boston Park Rangers (tel. 617/635–7383). The former's run mid-April–November, the latter's June–October. Several other organizations offer tours (fee required). Colonial costumed guides (tel. 617/227–8800) lead tours June through August and will also arrange private tours. Little Feet Tours (77 N. Washington St., tel. 617/367–3766) are geared for children 6–12. You can also contact the Boston Park Rangers about the free Haunt Jaunt (10-person minimum), a scavenger hunt through the Granary Burying Ground.

Boston Common to the Bunker Hill Monument

 617/242-5642 National Park Service, 617/227-8800
Freedom Trail Foundation; www.thefreedomtrail.org,
www.cityofboston.gov/parks

 Trail free; some
attractions charge

Attraction hrs vary,
most daily 9-5

 8 and up

Charlestown. Highlights for most kids include the three burying grounds, such as the Granary,
where you'll find headstones for such famous patriots as Paul Revere and Samuel Adams.

You can make the whole adventure (at least 4½ hours) into a badge-earning mission by
picking up the free Junior Ranger Pack from either of the National Park Service visitor
centers: downtown at 15 State Street (across from the Old State House) or at the
Charlestown Navy Yard. Complete the activities and return them to either office for your
official Junior Ranger Badge. Another kid-friendly activity is the park service's Hit the
Trail Passport (95¢), which has a space for a stamp from every stop.

To save the tired dogs, hop either the water shuttle (Pier 4, $1 per person) back to
downtown Boston or the Orange Line from the Community College station to the
Back Bay.

HEY, KIDS! Legend has it that Mother Goose is buried in the Granary Burying Ground. Locals believe that Elizabeth Goose, who got her name
from her husband, Isaac Goose (formerly VerGoose), was the famous storyteller.
She is supposed to have concocted the rhymes to entertain her 20 children
and stepchildren. Her grave lies on the north side of the burying ground
(check map at the gate), but remember that rubbings are not allowed.

GEORGE'S ISLAND

If you're coming to George's Island for the first time, you may well wonder, "Who's George?" It's a good question. Though documents attribute the name to Capt. John George, historians disagree about whether the island's moniker actually predates the 18th-century Boston merchant (island records date from as far as 1690). Nevertheless, historic discord can't mar the island's inherent charms. Seven miles from downtown, the island of the mysterious George is one of the most popular—and serene—spots in Boston Harbor. Home to a 19th-century fort, the parcel of land combines the best parts of outdoor adventuring: fresh air, great views, and incomparable historic exploration.

Most notable is stately Ft. Warren, whose massive, 150-year-old granite walls stand about 30 feet high and 8 feet thick. The 10-acre military structure was used from the Civil War until the end of World War II. Unlike Ft. Warren's former "guests" (i.e., Confederate prisoners), today's visitors have their run of the place. You can storm the parade grounds (the grassy area inside fortress walls), climb into the two observation towers, and poke

KEEP IN MIND Water service to the island is provided from Hingham and other locations in addition to Boston; ask Boston Harbor Cruises for details. You can also hop a free water taxi (tel. 617/223–8666) to some of the other islands in the Boston Harbor Island State Park/National Recreation Area (Peddock's, Lovell's, Grape, Bumpkin, and Gallops), but you'll have to return to George's to catch the boat home. During summer, free ranger-led fort tours are offered several times daily. Inquire at the information booth at the dock or with the Metropolitan District Commission (tel. 617/727–5290), which also provides information on summer Civil War reenactments and other events.

Departures: 63 Long Wharf

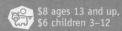 $8 ages 13 and up,
$6 children 3–12

 Late Apr–mid-June and early Sept–mid-Oct.,
departures daily 10, 12, 2, and 4; mid-June–
early Sept, departures daily 10–5, hourly

617/227–4321 Boston Harbor Cruises, 617/727–7676 state
park, 617/223–8666 info line; www.bostonislands.com

 All ages

around the long-deserted casemates (living and artillery compartments) and abandoned gun batteries. The truly observant might be able to discern the purpose of some compartments. Brick ovens, for example, signal that you're in the bakery; the small wood-lined rooms were probably powder magazines. You might even spot a remnant of combat—the purported impression of a cannonball—in a cracked walkway outside Bastion D. Also keep an eye out for the ghost of the lady in black. Historians declare it hogwash—most likely the creation of storyteller Edward Rowe Snow—but some believe the long-dead wife of a Confederate prisoner inhabits the island to this day.

A walk along the seawall and tidal pools are other pleasant ways to enjoy an afternoon. Just leave the starfish and other wildlife for future visitors to discover. You're welcome to toss a ball or a Frisbee or imagine yourself a soldier stationed here during WWII, passing the time with a game of baseball.

HEY, KIDS! What the heck is a sally port? The girlish name refers to a fort's main entrance (from the French for "leaving gate"). Other strange names include the demi-lune (the half-moon-shape building on the fort's north) and the scarp gallery (Bastion E), where musket-toting soldiers stood guard.

EATS FOR KIDS The best way to appreciate the splendor of George's Island is to dine alfresco, as picnics are welcome. If you left the cooler at home, you can grab simple eats (hot dogs, burgers, etc.) at the seasonal on-site **snack bar,** near the dock. There are also snack bars on board the boats that bring you here. Despite its name, the **Dockside Restaurant & Sports Bar** (183 State St., tel. 617/723–7050), outside Faneuil Hall, does have a children's menu.

HAMMOND CASTLE

What to get one's wife for a wedding present? If you were John Hays Hammond, Jr., something as mundane as a toaster just wouldn't do. So in 1926, the wealthy inventor began construction of an imposing medieval castle to present to his new bride.

Today the seaside palace lives on as a tourist mecca and museum. That its builder was inspired by English castles (Hammond lived across the pond as a boy) is obvious in the details. From its drawbridge (alas, it doesn't go up) to the stained-glass windows, this is every bit the royal abode. True, its early 20th-century origins make it a few hundred years late to be truly medieval, but Hammond did a remarkably good job infusing his mansion with authenticity. The end result has Knights of the Round Table written all over it.

Self-guided tours of the structure take roughly an hour, though you're welcome to stay as long as you like. Follow the passageways to eight of the castle's most splendid

HEY, KIDS!
Next time you flip on the TV from across the room, think of Mr. Hammond. The holder of more than 400 patents, the inventor is known for his radio-operated gizmos and is lauded as the father of remote control.

KEEP IN MIND As regal as she is, Hammond Castle is imposing enough to be downright frightening to some kids. Tight spiral staircases make good shoes a must, and the castle is not handicapped accessible. Look for special events throughout the year, including King Arthur's Faire in April, Robin Hood's Faire in July, and some ultra-ultra-spooky Halloween events during the end of October and beginning of November—too scary for some kids.

rooms, including the great hall, the Renaissance dining room, and two guest bedrooms. The glass-roofed indoor courtyard, featuring a naturally landscaped pool and lots of greenery, was designed so Hammond could enjoy swimming as if in the great outdoors. He could even create indoor weather, such as rain and fog. Another favorite room, the library has a ceiling designed to allow whispered conversations in one corner to be deciphered clear across the room—intended to thwart secrets during Mr. Hammond's business meetings. It might make you wish for such a setup during your children's teenage years. Outside the castle walls—where the Atlantic Ocean makes for one spectacular backdrop—is pretty remarkable as well.

As fascinating as it is, Hammond Castle is a look-but-don't-touch kind of place, and proper lord and lady manners are required. In other words, no running or screaming. But that doesn't seem to weigh too heavily on little ones, who get caught up in their own imaginations.

EATS FOR KIDS Picnicking is not allowed at the castle, but you can dine outdoors at nearby Stage Fort Park, which is also a great place to run off some steam. The **Pilot House** (3 Porter St., tel. 978/283–0131) serves up tasty barbecue. Get pizza, subs, and such at **Steve's Family Restaurant** (24 Railroad Ave., tel. 978/283–4227).

HARVARD MUSEUM OF NATURAL HISTORY

Leave it to the folks at Harvard to find a way around the laws of physics. This group of natural history museums may look finite on the outside, but inside it seems to go on forever. (Too bad they haven't found a way around the parking nightmare; do yourself a favor and take public transportation.)

Ultracool exhibits have made the rambling Harvard halls a kid favorite. Three separate museums make up the place: the Botanical Museum, the Museum of Comparative Zoology, and the Mineralogical and Geological Museum. This last one showcases Mother Nature's baubles in display-case-filled rooms that resemble the world's largest jewelry store. More fascinating still is the meteor exhibit, featuring great slabs of space debris that have fallen to earth—some thousands of years old.

There's more ancient history in the Museum of Comparative Zoology. Dino-loving kids will have a field day exploring the jumbo prehistoric leftovers, including a plateosaurus from

EATS FOR KIDS An old institution in Harvard Square, **Charlie's Kitchen** (10 Elliott St., tel. 617/492–9646) is known among locals for burgers—particularly double cheese-burgers. Around the corner from the museum, **Bertucci's** (21 Brattle St., tel. 617/864–4748) isn't as colorful, but it has dependable pizza and other Italian fare. Or try out the Mexican food at the **Border Cafe** (32 Church St., tel. 617/864–6100).

the Triassic period and an elephant-size mastodon from...New Jersey. Another highlight is the mind-boggling collection of taxidermic animals, which your kids will either love or hate depending on their stance on animal rights. For the record, these specimens—including tigers, bears, and whales—were collected over a century ago, when people felt differently about such things. Regardless, the proximity you can get to these creatures is breathtaking. Suffice it to say that it'll be the closest you ever get (hopefully, anyway) to a lion's mouth.

In between these two galleries is the Botanical Museum, which might seem ho-hum until you take a closer look. Display cases contain thousands of incredible flower reproductions, lifelike right down to the insects. Fashioned as educational tools between 1887 and 1936 (colorful textbooks didn't exist 100 years ago), the world-famous Glass Flowers collection of replicas is made entirely of glass; many people walk by a time or two before realizing they're fakes.

HEY, KIDS! Look up when walking through the Great Mammal Hall. There, dangling two stories above you, are several actual skeletons of giant whales. Those hairy-looking things hanging near their mouths are not mustaches, but baleens. Whales use them to filter food particles from water for noshing.

KEEP IN MIND On weekends, look around the building for Creature Features, live animal presentations. The structure housing the natural history museum also houses the Peabody Museum of Archaeology and Ethnology, containing cultural artifacts from around the world. Kids' reactions to this museum are usually less animated than to the zoology museum, however, so upon entering the building, turn left.

HIGGINS ARMORY MUSEUM

You'd expect to find a medieval castle in England—but in *New* England? Sure, it looks like an ordinary office building on the outside (completed in 1931, it was one of the first glass and steel buildings in this country), but inside is anything but ordinary. A reproduction of a 13th-century European castle, Higgins Armory is uncannily authentic, from its "stone" walls (really plaster) right down to its painstakingly applied faux age marks.

The late John Woodman Higgins built the palace to house his enormous collection of armor. The ultimate fan of steel, the metal magnate traveled the world collecting, amassing an assortment that dates from the days of the gladiators. In this stronghold, you'll encounter all the trappings of the Round Table denizens, not to mention the all-important coat of arms for their horses. All that's missing are the gallant knights themselves.

EATS FOR KIDS Friendly, family-owned **Barbers Crossing** (325 W. Boylston St., tel. 508/852–3435) specializes in seafood, but a children's menu covers hot dogs, spaghetti, and the like. A short walk away, tasty **Eddy's Pub, Pizza and Deli** (317 W. Boylston St., tel. 508/853–2269) serves the kind of fare it's named for.

HEY, KIDS! Ever wonder what it was like to live in a medieval castle? Here's one rule: children were not allowed to eat in the formal dining room until they had mastered proper table manners. That meant eating only with the thumb, pointer, and middle finger of your right hand (southpaws had their left hands bound so they wouldn't forget). Sound severe? Well, there were some good points, too. You never got yelled at for wiping your hands on the tablecloth; napkins hadn't been invented yet.

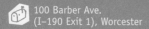
100 Barber Ave.
(I-190 Exit 1), Worcester

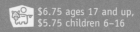
$6.75 ages 17 and up,
$5.75 children 6-16

T-Sa 10-4, Su 12-4

508/853-6015; www.higgins.org

5 and up

Suits of armor are spread over four floors. Plaques point out important details, such as how you can tell the difference between battle armor and jousting armor (the latter has a "target" plate over the left shoulder). On-site staff members are more than happy to answer questions. You might wonder, for example, why some of the armor is so ornate. "It's clothing," explains one staffer. "In addition to being protected, knights wanted to look cool."

Though the ambience is fantasy-inspiring, the no-touch aspect can make the Higgins a snooze to some kids, especially those used to interactive exhibits. Fortunately, the Higgins has those, too. A second-floor discovery center features kid-size lord and lady apparel to wear, as well as a few helmets to try on (they are h-e-a-v-y). If you're squeamish about sharing headgear with the entire court, get the knight's-eye view by putting your kisser up to a face plate mounted inside a block. Other activities include period games and occasional craft projects.

KEEP IN MIND Demonstrations—during which some audience members might be asked to try on some of the weighty duds—take place twice daily in the auditorium on weekends and during school vacations. Weekends, look for a live knight, Joan of Arc, or a performance group reenacting the life of a knight and his peeps (AKA entourage). As for equipping yourself: leave the enormous backpacks at home. Pieces of Higgins's collection have walked off (figuratively speaking) over the years, and the armory has had to respond by prohibiting big bags.

JOHN F. KENNEDY LIBRARY AND MUSEUM

Let's face it. As hard (and depressing!) as it is to believe, the Kennedy administration registers as much like ancient history to today's children as the Roosevelt administration does to us adults. Yet nearly four decades after its untimely end, John F. Kennedy's brief term in the White House continues to read more like a fable than political history. True, some of the rosy details have shown a few thorns over the years, but the story of the handsome politician and his beautiful bride has lost little luster, remaining a captivating historical moment to be discovered at the Kennedy Library.

Start your visit with a 17-minute film that introduces you to the brash young senator, from the beginning of his meteoric rise right up to his 1960 nomination to the Democratic presidential ticket. The exhibits that follow represent a time line of the ensuing years, telling stories through props, film clips, front pages, and photos.

That Mr. Kennedy was the country's first media president is displayed vividly through numerous

HEY, KIDS! You'll learn all sorts of interesting things about Kennedy and about people here. For instance, JFK's charisma made him one of the country's most popular presidents, which might lead you to believe that he won the 1960 election by a landslide. In reality, the 43-year-old Kennedy (the youngest president ever elected) received only 118,550 votes (just .2% of those voting) more than future president Richard Nixon. By the middle of Kennedy's term in office, however, he was so popular that *well* over half the country claimed to have voted for him.

Columbia Point (I–93 Exit 15)

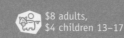 $8 adults,
$4 children 13–17

Daily 9–5

617/929–4500; www.jfklibrary.org

10 and up

video snippets. The president held 63 press conferences during his short term in the White House, cementing his image in the public memory and revolutionizing the amount of access the nation had (and continues to have) to its highest public officer. Features of the tour—including some re-created areas of the White House, and handwritten notes and letters—provide fascinating glimpses into the era, educating in an amiable, accessible manner. Jacqueline admirers will find the former first lady well represented, too; look for some of her notes and photos, as well as a pillbox hat or two.

Don't miss a visit to the Situation Theater, where videos replay anxious moments from the Cuban Missile Crisis, when the threat of the atomic bomb loomed in our backyard. The footage provides a chilling reminder of the specter of nuclear war.

EATS FOR KIDS
At the cafeteria-style **Museum Cafe,** the food won't bowl you over, but the setting—overlooking the pavilion—is pleasant. **Phillips Old Colony House** (780 Morrissey Blvd., tel. 617/ 282–7700) is easy to reach and easy on your kids; it's got salads, sandwiches, steaks, and a nice-size children's menu.

KEEP IN MIND The library is best for schoolkids familiar with this period in history. If you're bringing younger students, pick up the "Treasures of the Kennedy Library" guide, outlining a scavenger hunt of sorts through the museum. Also make time to appreciate the stellar views of the city across the water. The dramatic glass pavilion atrium is a poignant tribute to Kennedy and a lovely place to watch the world go by. To get closer to the water, descend steps outside the building. From May to November, look for JFK's *Victura,* a sloop given to him when he was 15, docked outside.

LE GRAND DAVID & HIS OWN SPECTACULAR MAGIC COMPANY

Copperfield, Shmopperfield. Who needs *that* David when the North Shore town of Beverly gives you this one (dramatically pronounced Da–veed). True, you won't see vanishing jets or disappearing sphinxes, but what you do get is humor, fun, and a little bit of good old-fashioned prestidigitation. And from your seat in this intimate theater, you won't need high-power binoculars to see.

Nearly everything about this charming show is a throwback, from the glittery costumes to the handsome barbershop quartet. A dashing, tuxedoed usher welcomes you in, player-piano music tinkles in the lobby, and Harlequin-attired jugglers entertain as you await the rise of the curtain. The company itself—headed by elder statesman Marco the Magi (Cesareo Pelaez), not by David, who is also a leading player—thinks of its style as "classic." The theater is similarly well aged. Built in 1920 by a pair of vaudeville-era entertainers, the palace has been lovingly restored by the Grand David troop, who purchased it back in 1977.

HEY, KIDS!
To become a magical legend, you need more than stellar sleight of hand. You need time. The Grand David company has been performing for more than a quarter century, appearing in *Guinness World Records* as the "longest-running resident stage magic production/show." Now that's magic!

KEEP IN MIND Tickets for the show are often available the same day, as the Cabot Street Cinema Theatre holds 700 seats. However, since there is no reserved seating, it's best to show up 30 minutes before the show starts as the best spots fill up early. If parking can't be found on the street, you can find spaces in a municipal lot around the corner. The company's other show, "An Anthology of Stage Magic," is also good for kids; it's performed at 2 on sporadic Saturdays, October–May, at the nearby Larcom Theater.

Cabot St. Cinema Theatre,
286 Cabot St., Beverly

 978/927–3677

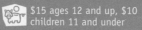 $15 ages 12 and up, $10
children 11 and under

🕐 Mid-Sept–July, Su 3

🛒 All ages

Perhaps the greatest piece of magic is how the troop maintains the scope of the show. A self-supporting company, the players construct their own props, dress their own stage, and sew their own costumes—the latter a particularly daunting task since dozens of players make myriad wardrobe changes in every performance. That isn't to say that the finished product looks homemade. True, there is a homespun quality to the extended-family troop's performance style, and there's a hint of the hokey along with the dramatic. But the illusions will leave you scratching your head, and performers and stagehands pull it all off with aplomb, a fact evidenced by the hundreds of spectators who visit each week.

Great fun as the show is, do consider your child's age and disposition before buying tickets. At roughly 2¼ hours (with an intermission), the show may be too long for really little ones.

EATS FOR KIDS The theater's old-style ambience is finished off with an upstairs **café** featuring yummy cookies and baked goods, just like homemade. That's not the best news for parents, since snacking during the late-afternoon show can do in an appetite for dinner. If you are hungry, the **Cabot Place Restaurant** (256 Cabot St., tel. 978/927–3920) has light (soups and salads) and heavier (seafood casseroles and Newburgs) fare as well as a children's menu. Homemade Italian favorites are on hand at **Cafe Salerno** (73 Cabot St., tel. 978/927–1979).

LIBERTY FLEET OF TALL SHIPS

Centuries after being dethroned as the most efficient form of transoceanic transportation, the tall ship has reemerged as a beloved form of aquatic transit. And it's no wonder. These gallant ladies are a sight, drawing contented sighs as their billowing sails pass on the horizon and earning a place in the sailing public's heart.

Boston families without the wherewithal to actually own one of these esteemed ladies (or the gastrointestinal constitution to embark on a multiday ocean voyage) needn't remain mere spectators. Each spring, the Liberty Fleet's two sizable schooners arrive in Boston from their winter port in Key West, Florida, and invite visitors aboard for two hours of tall-ship sailing splendor.

Prospective mateys can choose from two schooners: the 125-foot *Liberty Clipper* or the 80-foot *Liberty*. Both are accurate replicas of two-masted, 18th-century fishing vessels, the kind you would have seen tooling around the nation's coastlines more than 100 years ago.

67 Long Wharf

 617/742-0333;
www.libertyfleet.com

 $30 ages 13 and up,
$18 children 12 and
under; Su brunch $45
ages 13 and up,
$25 children

 Memorial Day–Sept, daily 12,
3, and 6 plus Su 11

 All ages

Daily voyages depart Long Wharf for scenic tours of Boston Harbor. Precisely where you'll go varies each day; this is a sailing ship, after all. "It all depends on which way the wind blows," declares a crew member. If you're not content to merely sit on the sidelines feeling the wind in your hair (although there's a lot to be said for this), you're welcome to pitch in as an honorary crew member and help hoist the sails, an onerous task that requires abundant hands on deck. Of course, the ship needs to be steered, too, and little ones are often invited to try their hand at the helm. And since this is a pleasure cruise, you needn't worry about being ordered to swab the deck.

KEEP IN MIND
Reservations for all sails are essential, as are plenty of sunscreen and a light sweater. Breezes on the open sea can chill passengers even on a sultry day.

HEY, KIDS! Experienced seafarers speak in a language all their own. "Charley Noble," for example, is not a "who" but rather a "what"; it's actually the galley stovepipe. (Remember this if someone ever sends you to go find "him.") "Avast," as in "Avast ye mateys," means "stop what you're doing." "Ahoy" is a call to attract attention, and "Aargh," is, well, self-explanatory.

MAKE WAY FOR DUCKLINGS TOUR

F olks outside New England may consider a certain quacker down in Orlando to be the world's most notable waterfowl. Among Bostonians, however, there are no ducks more famous than those in the Mallard family.

As most anyone over the age of 3 knows, the Mallards are the title characters in Robert McCloskey's famed children's book *Make Way for Ducklings*. On the hunt for a home, Mrs. Mallard and her clan of eight—Jack, Kack, Lack, Mack, Nack, Ouack, Pack, and Quack—hold up traffic as they endeavor to cross a busy Boston street. (Those who've been pedestrians in this city can attest that there is no higher drama than that.)

Walking in the Mallards' web prints begins at the visitor center on the Boston Common. Travelers first get a quick refresher course on the story and then a bit of history of the Common. Most sights on the 1½-hour trip (reservations absolutely required) appear

EATS FOR KIDS Weekdays, **Cosi Sandwich Bar** (53 State St., tel. 617/723–3369) has to-die-for flat bread and yummy fillings (caramelized onions, etc.) that will please adults but might raise kids' eyebrows. Not far, in the Back Bay, **T.G.I. Friday's** (26 Exeter St., tel. 617/266–9040) has dependable kids' staples.

KEEP IN MIND Though tour guides carry a copy of the book, they don't often read from it along the way, so it's not a bad idea to bring a copy for your own reference. Each Mother's Day, Historic Neighborhoods celebrates the story with Ducklings Day. Tourists, many dressed up as their favorite characters, gather on the Common and proceed to parade (no tour this day) through Beacon Hill back to the Public Garden, where there is entertainment and snacks. Tickets are $15 in advance for a family of four.

Historic Neighborhoods: 99 Bedford St.;
tour start: Boston Common visitor center

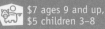 $7 ages 9 and up,
$5 children 3–8

 Late June–Aug, F–Sa 11

617/426–1885; www.historic-
neighborhoods.org

6 and up

just the way they did in McCloskey's drawings. These include the State House on Beacon Hill, Louisburg Square, and the building that was the Old Corner Bookstore. Though it's now a 7-11, most kids can easily recognize it from its unique design. (Tour guides are experts in city architecture and lore and ably build in a bit of age-appropriate history, encouraging kids to recognize different designs in Boston's landmarks.) The tour winds down at the Public Garden, which you'll enter, just as Mrs. Mallard did, through the gate on the corner of Beacon Street. Bronze casts of some of the Mallard clan provide a fitting final stop.

Historic Neighborhoods, the nonprofit group that runs the tour, does its best to remain true to the story, but certain liberties are taken. Mr. and Mrs. Mallard actually flew *over* the Beacon Hill State House. For obvious reasons, however, you'll have to be content to walk through.

HEY, KIDS! How did Robert McCloskey draw so accurately? The author was once a budding artist attending classes at Vesper George Art School, right in Boston. During his apprentice days, McCloskey made drawings while gazing out the window of his apartment near Louisburg Square. Who said daydreaming is a waste of time? Be sure to ask about McCloskey's apartment on the tour.

MINUTE MAN NATIONAL HISTORICAL PARK

Grab a bike, a stroller, or just a pair of sneakers and follow the tracks of the Revolutionary War. Though the history is secondary to the fun, it's hard not to be drawn in. Markers all along the way tell the story of Colonial soldiers who took on the English on this very spot several hundred years ago—April 19, 1775, to be precise.

Bikers, walkers, and runners love the Battle Road trail, spanning 900 acres of the park. The longest continuous off-road stretch runs 5½ miles between the Minute Man Visitor Center and Meriam's Corner. The 11-mile round-trip is perfect for young cyclists. Except for one place where it crosses a busy section of Route 2, the trail has no automobile traffic to contend with and relatively flat terrain.

Many people recommend starting at the new Minute Man Visitor Center, in Lexington, where a 30-minute multimedia presentation—"Road to Revolution"—orients you to what's ahead. This might work well in season, when such attractions as the Hartwell Tavern (open mid-

KEEP IN MIND Don't get the park confused with the Minuteman Commuter Bikeway, which can have intimidating weekend crowds. (Note that the Battle Road trail can fill up on summer weekends, too.) To appreciate the park's solemnity, come off-season. Look for parking signs on major roads, and pick up trail maps at either visitor center. Reenactments are held each Patriots Day weekend, and other events take place year-round (call tel. 978/369-6993 for a schedule). Two good spots to learn about local and American history are the Concord Museum (200 Lexington Rd., Concord, tel. 978/369-9609) and the Museum of Our National Heritage (33 Marrett Rd., Lexington, tel. 781/861-6559).

Minute Man Visitor Center:
Rte. 2A, Lexington

Visitor centers
free; some historic
sites charge

Daily sunrise–sunset; visitor centers
May–Oct, daily 9–5; Nov–Apr, daily 9–4

978/369–6993 or 781/862–7753;
www.nps.gov/mima

All ages

May–October, with costumed interpreters but no grub and ale!) and the Wayside Home of Authors (home to Louisa May Alcott and Nathaniel Hawthorne and a safe harbor for slaves traveling the Underground Railroad) are open. But during the off-season, the reverse approach might be even better. Starting at Meriam's Corner means you'll reach the visitor center at the midpoint of your round-trip. The film and that all-important pit stop (the latter being particularly important since there are no other bathrooms along the way) will help you recharge for the trip back. Bring along a snack (a good idea since food services do not exist along the route), and enjoy it at the outdoor picnic tables. The only potential hitch in this approach is that the small Meriam's Corner parking lot tends to fill up on peak days.

Though you'll have to drive there, the North Bridge is worth a visit as well. To really get the kids into the history, ask at one of the visitor centers about the Junior Ranger Activity Booklet ($1.50).

EATS FOR KIDS
Ice cream and a huge menu await at the surprisingly quaint **Brigham's Ice Cream** (15 Main St., Concord, tel. 978/369–9885), west of the park. Other options include **Bertucci's** (1777 Massachusetts Ave., Lexington, tel. 781/860–9000), **Country Kitchen** (181 Sudbury Rd., Concord, tel. 978/371–0181), and suggestions under Walden Pond.

HEY, KIDS! The first shots of April 19—the inaugural day of the American Revolution—were fired early in the morning on the Lexington Green. However, historians cite the North Bridge encounter as the official beginning of the conflict. It was there that Ralph Waldo Emerson's "shot heard round the world" was fired and the first British soldiers fell.

MUSEUM OF FINE ARTS

Who says art appreciation is just about looking? While the preeminent image of the art world may be of echoing corridors and sacrosanct vestibules, more and more museums—like this one—are getting away from the whole "hallowed halls" thing. Says one MFA staff member, "It's hard to consider our halls hallowed when we've got kids running around with glue and ink in their hands."

Such art supplies are available in abundance through the MFA's Family Place, which offers weekend school-year workshops that let kids experiment with art as well as appreciate it. (Families touring on their own should not bring glue and ink, however.) Brightly colored kits distributed through the program have particular themes. Walk among the art, and then try your hand in the downstairs workshop. Pamphlets guide you to the appropriate gallery and even suggest follow-up reading materials. Themes change each weekend, and materials change with each theme. Elaborate activities continue daily during school vacation weeks; a Hats and Headdresses project, for example, ran in conjunction with an exhibit of

HEY, KIDS!
Try your hand at the masters. The MFA encourages you to bring pencils and pads (maximum size 18"x 24") and to try and sketch some of these magnificent pieces of art.

KEEP IN MIND Family Place is held October–June, Saturday and Sunday 11–4. During Boston schools' February and April breaks, activities are offered Monday–Friday 10–4. Children's Room programs are held 3:30–4:45, Monday–Friday (September–June) and Monday–Thursday (July–August). To participate in any of these drop-in programs, check in at the front desk at the West Wing entrance on arrival. Family Night Out, Wednesdays 5:30–8:30 in July and August, is similar to Family Place but has more activities. There are special teen programs, too.

tiaras. Art Alive, given Saturday afternoons (times vary), might feature a theatrical performance or book reading.

Of course, you can make forays on your own any day. Pick up one of the "Paper Guides" from the Sharf Information Desk at the West Wing entrance; these two-page pamphlets detail particular exhibits and proffer scavenger-hunt-type explorations. Kids who'd truly like to explore the museum on their own—in other words, without you—can do so at the Children's Room. The free, after-school drop-off program (for children 6–12) features supervised museum exploration and art workshops.

To make budding art lovers less reluctant, experts suggest focusing on one gallery (a good idea since this museum is B-I-G) and avoiding weekends. Also check out the museum shop. Though you'll have to navigate around some typical souvenir-y items (accordion anyone?), there are some exceptional kid-oriented art books.

EATS FOR KIDS There are four restaurants at the museum. The most appropriate—i.e., the one with hot dogs and sandwiches—is the **Courtyard Café.** Off property, continue the adventure with Thai food at the **Brown Sugar Cafe** (129 Jersey St., tel. 617/266–2928). If it's grill fare you're after, try **Thorntons Fenway Grill** (100 Peterborough St., tel. 617/421–0104).

MUSEUM OF SCIENCE

Think of this spiffy institution in the eponymous Science Park as an arcade for your brain. There are gadgets and gizmos aplenty, but each is designed to teach you something more than how to maximize your Super Mario score. The museum claims roots back more than a century and a half, but this is no dinosaur. Interactive exhibits here—and there are more than 600 of them—are state-of-the-art, and you don't need to be a mini Albert Einstein to appreciate them. Novel concepts engage even the science-phobe.

Three floors offer a dizzying number of exhibits—too many to take in on one visit. Swings and seesaws provide the structure for learning about fulcrums and gravity in Science in the Park. Optical illusions will bowl you over in Seeing is Deceiving. Kids can spend hours bounding up and down the musical stairs in the Red Wing atrium. Successive 20-foot models of a Tyrannosaurus rex have been time-honored kid-favorites, but the latest version has been updated for accuracy. The 3-D Virtual Fish Tank, where you can create computer-generated fish—and then instruct them to eat your friends' fish—is positively addictive.

HEY, KIDS! Don't wait for a thunderstorm to appreciate the power of lightning. The "Lightning" show at the Theater of Electricity gets you remarkably close to this striking phenomenon. It's much safer than Ben Franklin's kite-and-key method, but loud sounds are not for the faint of heart. Watch a human guinea pig escape peril when the cage he's in is repeatedly struck by bolts of electricity. How does he survive? Electricity always follows the path of least resistance—in this case through the metal. The alternate demonstration—"Battle of the Currents"—is less lively, a little less loud, but also interesting.

No visit to the museum is complete without a visit to either (or both) the Mugar Omni Theater, which shows IMAX films, or the Charles Hayden Planetarium. Hourlong shows at the planetarium include "The Sky Tonight," detailing what to look for outside your door, and evening laser shows that many kids rate as awesome. Beautiful presentations and exceptionally entertaining hosts make the planetarium one of the museum's best spots and a good first stop any time you come.

Toddlers who can't appreciate the big-kid stuff can get a science primer at the Discovery Center. The 3,200-square-foot space has irresistible artifacts, such as an 18-foot python's skeleton, not to mention tons of experiments. Kids under 5 can try their hand at some water activities. There's even a soft-play corner for the smallest children.

EATS FOR KIDS
There's a whole universe of food available at the on-site **Galaxy Cafés,** which include the Starlite Deli, Pizza Gusta, and Galileo's. At the Cambridgeside Galleria, **Papa Razzi** (100 Cambridgeside Pl., Cambridge, tel. 617/577–0009) serves dependable pastas, pizzas, and more.

KEEP IN MIND The Museum of Science is big—really big. Biting off too much in one visit will probably leave you overwhelmed and under-satisfied. Web-browsing in advance can help you create a plan. Live presentations (such as the "Live Animal Show" and "Lightning") take place daily, so check the schedule when you arrive. If you're planning to see an IMAX show, call ahead and order tickets, particularly on weekends. If you're into astronomy, ask about Friday Night Stargazing, when the museum opens its observatory to the public, weather permitting (reservations recommended).

MUSEUM OF TRANSPORTATION

One of the world's earliest automobiles has a very sophisticated-sounding French name: the Charron-Giradot et Voigt. The nickname is much more pedestrian: the toilet car. Perhaps the predecessor to today's lanky recreational vehicles, this 1906 oddster came equipped with a fold-out bed, a sink, and a working commode underneath one of the jump seats. Just call it the antidote to stop-and-go traffic.

This rare automobile (there were only a handful made) is one of the more noteworthy vehicles in residence at the Museum of Transportation, a place that's bound to inspire curiosity in any kid who lights up when a classic automobile goes by. Dozens of colorful antiques (think *Chitty Chitty Bang Bang*) make up the collection, many dating from the turn of the last century. With most of these horseless carriages, you'll have to settle for just looking, though you can climb on the occasional exhibit.

HEY, KIDS!

Before the automobile, travelers relied on the good graces of equine transportation. Just like today's cars, these spiffy beauties required fuel—in the form of hay—and gave off toxic emissions—namely 20 pounds of manure each day.

KEEP IN MIND Before or after the museum, be sure to enjoy the rest of Larz Anderson Park, which includes a playground and romantic remnants of the old Anderson buildings, as well as some stellar views of Boston from the top of the hill. Weekends in summer, the museum hosts outdoor lawn events, such as the National Bicycle Show and Micro Mini Car Day, which feature food and activities. Call for a list of Family Sunday activities throughout the year.

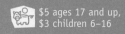

Two floors include numerous shiny old girls, and displays are rotated regularly. On any given day, you might come upon a 1908 Bailey Electric, a 1903 Gardner-Serpollet, or a 1901 Winton racing car. The interactive exhibit Kids on the Move heralds child-powered locomotion, including bikes (such as Boneshakers, those big-wheeled tricycles) and skates. A small children's room features rotating exhibits, crafts, and a wooden climb-on car representing the back end of a trolley.

The museum sits on the grounds of the larger Larz Anderson Park. Anderson and his wife, Isabelle, owned many of the cars on display here and once used the sprawling 64-acre property (which Isabelle willed to the town of Brookline upon her death in 1948) as a summer estate. The museum building was built to store the estate's original vehicles: horses and carriages. It's amazing to think that this castlelike structure—many times bigger than most palatial residences—was really just a glorified garage with servants' quarters.

EATS FOR KIDS In the park, there are some lovely pond-side areas that make for good picnicking grounds. **Legal Sea Foods** (43 Boylston St. [Rte. 9], Chestnut Hill, tel. 617/277–7300) offers plenty of choices from the sea. For tasty Italian specialties, try **Papa Razzi** (199 Boylston St., Chestnut Hill Mall, Chestnut Hill, tel. 617/527–6600).

NEW ENGLAND AQUARIUM

There are lots of good reasons to visit Boston's Central Wharf. Myrtle is one of the best. At 600 pounds, she's a sizable lady—green head, thick shell, and all.

Myrtle, of course, is a sea turtle, a senior resident of the 30+-year-old New England Aquarium. Though she ranks as one of the most popular (and certainly one of the biggest) of the lot, she's in good company. She swims alongside more than 800 other sea creatures in the 200,000-gallon, four-story Ocean Tank that dominates the indoor landscape. You can view the action from virtually any angle, thanks to numerous windows and a ramp that spirals around the tank. It's simply hogfish heaven.

The rest of the aquarium features scads of denizens of the sea. Penguins cavort in the open-air rookery on the first floor. Seals engage visitors from their tank out front, while sea otters entertain guests out back. The third-floor Edge of the Water area lets you handle a few creatures, including starfish and horseshoe crabs. Interactive exhibits throughout teach

KEEP IN MIND Crowds make the dark, narrow confines of the aquarium tough to navigate. Good visiting times are Sunday before noon and after 1 during the week. (Avoid Saturday completely if you can.) Not only will you steer clear of crowds, but you'll cut your wait time to get in. Admission lines here are notoriously long, a particularly unwelcome circumstance in winter, since ticket booths are outside. Become a member, and skip the line completely. Or take a break in the Exploration Center, featuring interactive exhibits and an activity center; it's a quiet place to get away from it all.

about the ecology and conservation of the harbor, shore, and reef.

Yet another don't-miss highlight is Tyler. The lovable, irresistible 700-pound sea lion is the star of his own show on the permanently docked ship *Discovery*. He swims, slides, and even graces a lucky few with a fish-breath kiss. Like all other features here, the show is designed to educate, in this case demonstrating how human actions can be detrimental to nature. The lessons are well done, but Tyler is also simply a hoot to watch. In addition to being an acrobat, the lovable sea lion—along with his partner, Guthrie—are artistes, creating masterpieces (with brush in mouth) while you watch. The works are so stellar, they're actually sold in the gift shop (I kid you not). The facility's newest addition, an IMAX theater, has the biggest screen in New England and features 3-D effects (separate admission required). The aquarium also offers whale watches and other aquatic nature explorations.

EATS FOR KIDS
The on-site **Harbor View Café** features an adequate selection of burgers, hot dogs, sandwiches, and snacks. It may seem almost cannibalistic, but **Legal Sea Foods** (255 State St., tel. 617/742–5300) does have some of the best catches (broiled, fried, or baked) in town.

HEY, KIDS! How many different penguins can you identify? The penguin rookery has three types: African (classic black and white), rockhoppers (look for funny-looking yellow feathers on their heads), and little blues (tiny guys weighing no more than 2 pounds). Incidentally, the African variety is nicknamed the "jackass penguin" because of the braying sound it makes.

OLD NORTH CHURCH

L isten my children and you shall hear... of the poetic license of Henry Wadsworth Longfellow. It seems the famous poet, author of "Paul Revere's Ride," took a few liberties in his work. There were at least two other riders on that famous night—William Dawes and Samuel Prescott—but how many good rhymes are there for those names? As for "two if by sea," the sea was actually the Charles River, not the Atlantic Ocean, but "the river" would have thrown off the meter completely.

Still, the poem's "North Church tower"—the one where "a lantern aloft in the belfry arch" was hung—is authentic and still standing. Nearly 300 years old, the city's oldest church building still houses an active Episcopal congregation (it was built in 1723 as a Church of England) and is open daily for tours (self-guided in the off-season).

Inside, you'll be struck by the chapel's novel setup. The stately house of worship proffered Boston's first premium "box seats" (long before the FleetCenter) in the form of pew

EATS FOR KIDS The North End has some of the best Italian food around. Large portions and good prices at **La Famiglia** (112 Salem St., tel. 617/367–6711) have made it a family favorite. There's plenty more good Italian cooking at **Monica's** (143 Richmond St., tel. 617/720–5472).

KEEP IN MIND The Behind the Scenes tours run late June–August, and "Paul Revere Tonight" is offered from late June–October. Shows are given Thursday and Friday at 8, and tours are offered on the hour, weekdays 10–5, weekends 1–5. The church suspends sightseeing for Sunday services at 9 and 11; however, the public is welcome to attend. Listen for the hour-long peal of the church bells every Sunday at noon. To get more information about Paul Revere, stop by the famous patriot's house (19 North Sq., tel. 617/523–1676).

193 Salem St.

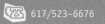 617/523–6676

 Donations requested; Behind the Scenes $8 adults, $5 children 18 and under; Paul Revere Tonight $12 adults, $8 children

 Daily 9–5; services Su 9 and 11

9 and up

boxes owned and occupied by local families. Pew fees paid for the church's upkeep, and the boxes' high walls kept parishioners sheltered from the cold sea breezes. Plaques outside the doors note the names of original owners.

Guests are welcome year-round, but the best time to visit is in summer, when the Behind the Scenes program is running. It's then that tour guides lead you down to the church crypts, where more than 1,000 people—mostly original church members—are interred. Then travel two flights up to the bell tower, where those famous lanterns were hung. Though the church is a decidedly low-tech attraction, kids familiar with this period of history will get into the historical significance, particularly when they realize they're walking the same steps traveled in 1775 by Robert Newman, the church sexton who signaled Paul Revere. Mr. Revere himself also appears in summer, in the family-friendly "Paul Revere Tonight," a one-hour nighttime show.

HEY, KIDS! Bells in the Old North Church (there are eight of them) were installed in 1745 and are still rung by hand. You can ask at the church about watching people ring the bells from 12 to 1 on Sunday (advance permission required). While you listen, remember that this is the oldest peal in North America.

OLD STATE HOUSE MUSEUM

What's a Boston landmark doing in Chicago? That's the question tourists would have been asking had the Windy City gotten its way and relocated the Old State House to the banks of Lake Michigan.

The building's brush with the Midwest is but one piece of its lore. First home to the state's government offices, the building was a pre-Revolution focal point. Anti-British rallies met here, the Boston Massacre seethed just outside (look for a circle of commemorative cobblestones in the street in front of the building), and local leaders read the Declaration of Independence, two weeks after its signing, from the second-floor balcony.

Government ranks outgrew the site and moved to the current State House, on Beacon Hill, in 1798. Temporarily deemed obsolete (explaining why it was nearly shipped off to Chicago), the building was snatched up in 1881 by the Bostonian Society, which maintains it today as a landmark and museum (though it's owned by the city).

KEEP IN MIND Visiting this stately structure will take about 40 minutes to an hour, with the most captivated audience being kids studying this period in history. Though John Hancock's groovy duds may momentarily impress some little ones (grade 1 or lower), most of the historic value will be lost on them. On March 5 each year, the anniversary of the Boston Massacre is commemorated with a reenactment. Call for details.

Detailed inside are tidbits about the evolution of the building and the city around it, and audio dramatizations recount significant events. Revolutionary relics include John Hancock's coat (check out those fancy duds!) and tea from the Boston Tea Party (donated by the family of tea-party participant Thomas Melvill, who found some leftover tea in his boot). Revolutionary War aside, one of the most fascinating displays tells of Boston's development, from a roughly square-mile peninsula, whose only mainland access was a narrow road, to a thriving metropolis that was exponentially enlarged with trainloads of fill. Upstairs in the Council Chamber, look for more artifacts from the Revolutionary War: muskets, bullet molds, and uniform accessories, to name a few. This is also where you can see (but not go out on) the balcony from which the Declaration was read. Rotating interactive exhibits tend to address more modern events, such as Boston after World War II. For kids, ask at the front desk for a handout that lets them explore the museum via a scavenger hunt.

HEY, KIDS! History's a great thing, but so is the subway meter. A red light shoots up each time a T (the Blue and Orange lines, if you're interested) rumbles below. Officially, the light is there to record the stress level on this historic structure. Between you and me, though, it's just really cool.

EATS FOR KIDS For something completely different, hike over to **Jacob Wirth** (31 Stuart St., tel. 617/338–8586), serving German specialties as well as traditional kid food. At Faneuil Hall, the **Salty Dog** (206 Faneuil Hall Marketplace, tel. 617/742–2094) has particularly good burgers and pub fare.

OLD STURBRIDGE VILLAGE

19

ong before frozen pizzas and personal CD players, families lived in communities such as Old Sturbridge. Spread over 200 acres, this enormous living-history museum offers a glimpse into the life of a 19th-century village.

Opened in 1946, the museum is the result of painstaking effort. Designers scoured New England to create a perfect hamlet, whose 40 buildings, transported from throughout the area, include stores, tradespeople's shops, a parsonage, a district school, and a number of elegant residences. All have been lovingly restored inside and out. The finished product is surreal in its picture-perfection, from the pristine steeple of the Meetinghouse to the white picket fence of the Fitch House.

Costumed interpreters further the old-fashioned effect. In their straw bonnets and stovepipe hats, a village's worth of residents go about their business, plowing fields, husking corn, and tending to their daily chores. Like the buildings, characters have

HEY, KIDS!
Think your classroom is small? If you went to school 100 years ago, you would have shared a one-room schoolhouse with students of all ages. Check out the re-created version here as well as other hands-on activities at the Samson's Children's Museum.

EATS FOR KIDS The brand-new **Tavern at Old Sturbridge** (village entrance, tel. 508/347–0395) serves modern fare (soups, salads, grills) in an "olde" atmosphere. At the village's **Bullard Tavern,** you can choose from a traditional midday buffet upstairs (with baked hams, meat pies, and such) or standard cafeteria fare (sandwiches and quiche) as well as some of the buffet offerings downstairs. Outside the village, the nearby **Picadilly Pub Restaurant** (362 Main St., tel. 508/347–8189) is a family favorite for chicken, fish, pastas, burgers, and probably just about anything else you can name.

1 Old Sturbridge Village Rd.
(I-90 Exit 9), Sturbridge

 $20 ages 16
and up, $10
children 6-15

 Jan–mid-Feb, Sa–Su 10–4, mid-Feb–Mar and Dec, Tu–Su
10–4; Apr–June and Sept–Oct, M–F 10–5, Sa–Su 10–6;
July–Aug, daily 10–6; Nov, daily 10–4

800/733-1830;
www.osv.org

 All ages

roots in actual history. For example, at Asa Knight's shop—an 1830s institution transplanted from Vermont—you may well find Asa himself behind the counter. Interpreters play their parts with aplomb, but there are some welcome limits: Old Sturbridge Village mercifully allows its 19th-century characters to answer questions in 21st-century English.

In addition to ambling among the day-to-day activities—a treat in and of itself—you can take part in special events. Among the village's hallmarks are Family Fun Days, held throughout the year: storytelling, sleigh rides, and candle-making are offered during winter school vacation, music and outdoor games in summer. Listen for fife and drums during the Independence Day observance, or get in on a traditional 1830s Thanksgiving. During the fall harvest, you can even get your hands dirty, helping to dig potatoes, shell beans, and husk corn. All that hard manual labor may just make you and your kids appreciate those frozen pizzas back home.

KEEP IN MIND You'll be walking a lot, mostly on dirt roads, so wear sturdy, comfortable shoes. There's probably too much to take in on one visit, a fact that's made easier to accept by passes that allow you to return the next day. Of course, that means you'll either have to drive back and forth or spend the night at a local hostelry. Two options that continue the historical adventure are the Old Sturbridge Village Lodges and the Oliver Wight House (U.S. 20, tel. 508/347-3327), both owned by the village.

OLD TOWN TROLLEY

Nothing screams "tourist" like a bevy of sightseers taking pictures out the window of a faux trolley car. Nevertheless, it's a shame that the folks who take advantage of this cute, albeit a little hokey, adventure are mostly out-of-towners. Tooling around in these orange and green, old-fashioned "trolleys" (buses, actually) is a kick for kids, not to mention a great education for anybody who wants to learn about Boston. Even better, the trip accommodates restless young ones by allowing you to hop on and off to visit attractions along the way (except, of course, for the last tour of the day).

The 100-minute tours cover much of Boston and a little bit of Cambridge. Vehicles take you to all the important landmarks—the historic Freedom Trail, Copley Square, and Faneuil Hall among them—and within a short T ride of others. Narration combines a little fact, a little legend, and a little lore, including such tidbits as which block is the city's most expensive (Louisburg Square) and what city garage was once condemned (Government Center's). You'll even get the lowdown on one of Boston's most popular nuptial spots; Trinity Church, the

KEEP IN MIND Local experts (i.e., hotel doormen) consider Old Town to have the best narration of the trolley tours. A nice bonus is that your ticket allows you to get on and off all day, even completing multiple circuits if you like. Other trolley tour operators include Beantown Trolley (tel. 617/236–2148), which also allows you unlimited circuits, and CityView (tel. 617/363–7899), which advertises the city's only "multimedia enhanced" trolley tour. The best place to compare maps is near the aquarium, where all these operators have kiosks.

story goes, has a wait list that goes on for years, prompting hopeful young women to sign on before they've nabbed (or even met!) the groom. It's called "eternal optimism," according to the tour. As you can see, congenial narrator/drivers can't help but have fun, and dialogue is heavy on shtick. A sound track includes the theme song from *Cheers* as you pass the Bull & Finch Pub and Ethel Merman singing about you-know-what business as you pass the theater district. It's all in good fun. Even the most cantankerous will have to work hard to keep from cracking a smile.

Technically, the circuit begins at the New England Aquarium (*see* #22), but you can board at any of the trolley's 16 stops. Don't have a ticket (good for two days)? No problem. Drivers will let you ride now and pay later at the first stop with a ticket booth. The company also offers a nighttime Ghosts & Gravestones Tour, as well as chocolate and holiday tours in winter.

EATS FOR KIDS Near the Northern Avenue Bridge, seafood-loving families can try the **Boston Sail Loft** (80 Atlantic Ave., tel. 617/227–7280) for tasty, dependable, and inexpensive food. In the Back Bay, **McCormick & Schmick's** (34 Columbus Ave., tel. 617/482–3999) is also known for its seafood. The **Harp** (85 Causeway St., tel. 617/742–1010) serves traditional favorites (fish-and-chips, burgers) with Irish flair. Also see restaurant suggestions for the Prudential Center Skywalk and many other Boston sights—wherever you happen to be around lunchtime.

PIRATE ADVENTURE

A h, the wonderful life of a pirate—the sailing, the salt air, the treasure, the robbing, pillaging, and plundering. Don't worry; it's only the first three you'll find on this fanciful adventure. A one-hour quest for pirate treasure on the open seas, this escapade provides about the best fantasy you'll find outside of Neverland.

The odyssey comes from the imagination of owner Than Drake, the self-proclaimed Captain Crisis, who built two ships (a second one launches from Orleans) expressly for the purpose of pirate play. Venturers from Hyannis cruise in the authentic-looking *Sea Gypsy*, a seemingly antique craft that is every bit the scalawag vessel, from the towering sail masts (they're a ruse—the ship is really a motorboat) to the cannons mounted on either side. Pirates-in-training get in the mood with a little facial decor, perhaps a painted-on eye patch or a twirly mustache. Everyone leaves his or her John Hancock (or Jean Laffitte) on the requisite pirate flag and helps hoist it into position. Then it's anchors aweigh.

HEY, KIDS!
Pretend pirates aren't the only ones who sailed these New England waters. Some very real scoundrels came through here as well. A few of the most notorious include William Kidd, Long John Avery, and the infamous Blackbeard. But don't worry. They're long gone.

KEEP IN MIND It's never too early to make a reservation (people start calling for July 4 bookings on April 1, the day the phone lines open). Boats will not travel in strong winds or thunderstorms but will voyage as scheduled in light rain. Cool breezes can bring a chill on a hot day, so bring a sweater. While you're in town, enjoy some of Hyannis's other pleasures, including the Cape Cod Potato Chip Factory Tour (100 Breed's Hill Rd., tel. 508/775-7253) or some time on a beach. The Orleans boat docks behind the Goose Hummock sports shop.

Ocean St. Dock, Slip 4, Hyannis

 $16.50 ages 3 and up, $12 children 2 and under

 508/430-0202; www.pirateadventurescapecod.com

🕐 Late June–Labor Day, M–Sa 9:30, 11, 12:30, 2, 3:30, and 5; Su 9:30, 11, and 12:30

🚼 3–10

Crew members plot the course based upon the "centuries-old" treasure map found on deck. To find the booty, you'll all have to keep a close eye out for clues—perhaps a floating bottle containing a message. There's peril as well; notorious scoundrel Pirate Pete appears bent on snagging the treasure for his very own. The threat is easily deflected with a blast from the super-powered cannons (ammunition: water). At last, "X" marks the spot of the treasure, and everyone lends a hand to haul it on board. There's no telling what you'll find—maybe doubloons. The festive trip home includes music and dancing and even a couple of rounds of the limbo. Once back at port, everyone gets a handful of booty to take home.

The *Sea Gypsy*'s small pirate crew—a captain and one other—runs the show from start to finish, interacting with little mateys all the way through. Parents can either join in or sit back and simply enjoy the ride.

EATS FOR KIDS The **Black Cat** (165 Ocean St., tel. 508/778–1233) seems a fitting place to dine after your pirate excursion. The tasty food is no pirate grub, though; it includes American grills and other specialties as well as a children's menu. In Hyannis, the **Olive Garden** (1095 Iyannough Rd., tel. 508/775–9896) has plenty of Italian fixings.

PLASTER FUN TIME

Artistic expression *and* immediate gratification—what more could a kid ask for? Drop into this paint-your-own-ceramics studio and create a spur-of-the-moment masterpiece. You can prime it, paint it, finish it, and, with no kiln-baking required, take it home the same day.

Budding artists pick from hundreds of pre-molded plaster sculptures, from the somewhat useless (animal statues and plaques) to the less cluttering (bookends, trinket boxes, pencil holders, and picture frames). Prices (and level of difficulty) are designated by shelf color; the red shelf is the cheapest ($7.99 each), purple the most expensive ($23.99). Of course you'll want to steer kids away from the individually priced items, such as the full-size columns ($90) and the 3-foot gargoyle ($200).

Once the piece is chosen (the most daunting part for kids), it's on to paint and brush. Ultra-friendly staff can be counted on for amiable coaching throughout the process, right

KEEP IN MIND The Dedham store is one of six Plaster Fun Time locations. The newest is in Braintree (121 Pearl St. tel. 781/849–8400). Others are in Natick (251 W. Central St., tel. 508/651–7673), Redding (347 Main St., tel. 781/944–6383), Salem (400 Highland Ave., tel. 978/745–7788), and Newton (118 Needham St., Newton Highlands, tel. 617/244–6080). Be sure to wear old clothes, as paint is likely to stain. Repeat customers should ask about "Frequent Painter" cards, which offer a free piece after you've paid for 12. This place is an absolute lifesaver during school vacations (when there are extended hours) and inclement weather.

691 Providence Hwy.
(Rte. 1 southbound), Dedham

781/326-4445;
www.plasterfuntime.com

$7.99 and up

M–F 11–7, Sa 10–7, Su 12–6

5 and up

from tying on the smocks (the rule is: no smock, no painting) to "fairy" dusting the finished product. Parents of little perfectionists will be happy to know that pre-dry mistakes can be instantly washed away. On the other hand, owner Nancy Selvaggi begs grown-ups to keep their hands off. "The whole idea is to let the kids be the creators," she says. Overzealous "helpers"—and we know who we are!—are best advised to get their own project. The final touch is a professionally applied spray that magically gives the piece a "baked" glow.

Prices include sculpture, primer, paints (as many colors as you want), and finish. The seemingly magical glitter (a secret in-house formula) is the hands-down favorite finishing touch. Lest anyone mistake this for a girls-only haven, check out the large supply of dinosaurs, skeletons, and swords, which has made art lovers out of many boys. Count on artists of both sexes to glow with pride over their newly minted creations.

HEY, KIDS! The paint's dry, but it's not exactly as you'd envisioned. Don't despair! Ask about the magical wax coating that can bring out all kinds of neat features on your work. To become famous, ask about getting a photo of your creation posted on the Web site.

EATS FOR KIDS It's not exactly the hometown institution implied by the name, but **Joe's American Bar & Grill** (985 Providence Hwy., tel. 781/329–0800) has a warm, cordial atmosphere and dishes to suit every taste, including the staples (ravioli and chicken fingers) on a vast children's menu. If you're heading north, you can't beat **Bertucci's** (683 VFW Pkwy., West Roxbury, tel. 617/327–0898) for great pizza and pasta. Also see Archery USA.

PLIMOTH PLANTATION

The year is 1627; the place is Plymouth, Massachusetts; and the townspeople are English settlers just arrived from the motherland. Just as those old historical films used to say, "You are there." Plimoth Plantation is a particularly engaging snippet of living history. What you'll find here is a re-creation of day-to-day village life in the early 17th century, complete with thatch-roofed homes (there are about 20 buildings in total), period tools, and conservatively clad Pilgrims.

"Residents," in fact, are what make this experience so enjoyable. The town's inhabitants actually represent real people, whose stories are drawn from long-ago diaries, transcripts, and letters. Researchers went as far as to travel to England to study their subjects' roots. Costumed interpreters—adorned in surprisingly un-Pilgrim-like garb (in other words, no black hats and buckled shoes)—play their roles with aplomb, rarely, if ever, veering from their parts. You'll have to listen carefully to understand them, however; as with the characters themselves, accents and dialects are carefully honed. And you'll have to choose

HEY, KIDS!
Do the Pilgrims' brand of livestock look a bit different than what you're used to? Farm animals here have been carefully bred to maintain their 17th-century appearance. One good example: all cows on the plantation, including the females, have horns.

KEEP IN MIND While at the plantation, visit the *Mayflower II*, a replica with costumed interpreters. The cost is $8 ages 13 and up, $6 children 6–12, and combination tickets with Plimoth Plantation are available. For a grand tour of the rest of the area, including that famous slab of history, Plymouth Rock, check out the Plymouth Rock Trolley Company (tel. 508/747–3419). Its 40-minute narrated excursions allow you to get off and on at the different sites. The company also does nighttime haunted Plymouth tours by lantern light under the name of Colonial Lantern Tour.

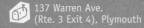
137 Warren Ave.
(Rte. 3 Exit 4), Plymouth

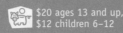
$20 ages 13 and up,
$12 children 6–12

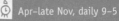
Apr–late Nov, daily 9–5

508/746–1622;
www.plimoth.org

All ages

your words carefully to get directions to the bathroom; however, Pilgrims *will* take mercy on children doing the "I have to go NOW" dance.

The first new exhibit in seven years—Thanksgiving: Memory, Myth, and Meaning—opened in 2002. So, as you might guess, English settlers aren't the only ones in town. At a nearby village dedicated to the Wampanoags, actual native people, dressed in traditional 17th-century native wear, answer questions about their people then and now.

The plantation is both fun and educational, and the Pilgrims manage to dispel a few myths. Contrary to popular impression, settlers weren't all somber. Just as today, the grim reapers were balanced by more boisterous folks. It may take a while to get into the 17th-century groove, and children may be taken aback by such greetings as "What cheer children? Have you come to help me in my labors?" But it's rewarding to interact with people so well versed in history, and so adept at making it interesting.

EATS FOR KIDS For home-style Italian, try **Mamma Mia's Restaurant** (122 Water St., tel. 508/747–4670). Outstanding comfort food, such as meat loaf and pork chops, has made the **Colonial** (39 Main St., tel. 508/746–0838) a hometown favorite, though it's closed on Thursday. Look for lots of seafood shacks a short walk away from the *Mayflower*.

PRUDENTIAL CENTER SKYWALK

One of Boston's most famous skyscrapers isn't exactly known for its beauty. Built in 1965, the Prudential is widely considered a blot on the Boston skyline. ("Its exterior looks like a car radiator," commented one local architect.) But like Furbys and trolls, the Prudential building—or the Pru, as it's known to locals—seems to have turned its very homeliness into one of the things that makes it so lovable. And the really good news is that if you're inside looking out, you don't have to see it at all.

Though it's relinquished its title as the city's tallest—that honor now belongs to the John Hancock Tower—the building nevertheless boasts remarkable views in all directions. (Sadly, due to security issues, the Hancock's observatory closed following the events of September 11, so the Pru currently offers the city's only public eagle's nest.) Zoom up the elevator to the 50th floor, and you'll be surrounded by vistas of the city and beyond. On a clear day, you can see all the way to Cape Cod. Low-key features accompanying the

KEEP IN MIND Since the Prudential doesn't provide brochures, bring a map to help you find your way around the view. Among the important landmarks you might see are Mt. Washington (the Northeast's tallest peak), to the north, and the tip of Cape Cod (Provincetown), to the southeast. To avoid confusing some of the Harbor Islands with Provincetown, look for the neck that connects it to the mainland. There are some pretty good views on the bottom floor, too, namely the store windows of the Pru's trendy shops (tel. 617/267–1002). Do yourself a favor and leave the credit cards at home.

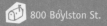
view include window graphics mapping out visible landmarks and several interesting displays that detail the city's past and present.

The Pru doesn't overtly embrace its status as a tourist attraction, a couple of coin-operated photo booths notwithstanding. There is nary a brochure to be found, and window graphics are a mite faded. But the subdued aura isn't necessarily a bad thing. You can actually get close enough to the windows to press your nose to the glass (theoretically, please—window washers hate that!). There are a couple of chairs sprinkled around, but inside window ledges make perfect window seats to sit peacefully and appreciate the view—almost like a visit to grandma's apartment. That the heating vents are mounted along these same ledges make them particularly warm, cozy spots for a winter's day.

HEY, KIDS! Question: which bridge out there is the "Salt and Pepper Bridge"? Answer: the Longfellow Bridge. Look closely. It's capped by structures that resemble the little condiment holders on your dining room table.

EATS FOR KIDS The international flair of **Restaurant Marché Mövenpick** (tel. 617/578–9700), right in the Prudential Center, is an adventure all by itself. Your choices include pasta, pizza, chicken, and just about anything else you can think of—all cooked right in front of you. The marketplace also has a vast food court featuring, among other things, **Rebecca's Cafe** (tel. 617/266–3355), known for its tasty sandwiches and salads. This is an office building, however, and the court gets extremely busy during business lunch hours.

PUPPET SHOWPLACE THEATRE

You'd think that such a low-tech diversion might fizzle when up against today's whiz-bang attractions. Not a chance. Though merchants have come and gone all around it, this little puppet-show-that-could has managed to hold its own despite the arrival of the high-tech generation.

Hiding behind a tiny storefront across from the Brookline Village T stop (blink and you could miss it), Puppet Showplace has been entertaining families for more than 25 years. No small-time sock-puppet organization here, this nonprofit group is professional through and through. In addition to staging its own performances, the company hosts occasional appearances by renowned puppeteers from all over the world. Over the years, guest artists have presented ethnic folk tales and original stories as well as stalwarts such as *Cinderella*. Puppet Showplace artist-in-residence Paul Vincent Davis is an internationally regarded

HEY, KIDS!
You don't need expensive store-bought puppets to create a puppet show at home. Even the pros use plain-old household objects sometimes. One company's nontraditional take on *Snow White* uses Prince rigatoni as the Prince, a Hunt's ketchup bottle as the Huntsman, and, playing the part of Snow White—a Hostess cupcake.

EATS FOR KIDS
Checkered tablecloths and huge portions of messy food are the order of the day at the **Village Smokehouse** (6–9 Harvard Sq., tel. 617/566–3782). The neighborhood hangout is right around the corner from the puppet theater (no, this is not the Harvard Square in Cambridge). Apart from the food, half the fun is watching the eats get cooked up center stage in the open pit. If barbecue doesn't suit your fancy, walk across the street from the theater for pizza and such at **Bertucci's** (4 Brookline Pl., tel. 617/731–2300).

 32 Station St., Brookline

 $8

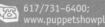 617/731-6400;
www.puppetshowplace.org

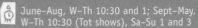 June–Aug, W–Th 10:30 and 1; Sept–May,
W–Th 10:30 (Tot shows), Sa–Su 1 and 3

5 and up; Tot shows 3–6

puppet master who has been performing here since 1977. He's known for his takes on classics, including *Rumplestiltskin* and *Beauty and the Beast,* and has been lauded for adapting folklore, such as his "Raccoon Tales," adapted from stories of the Seneca Native American tribes.

The Puppet Showplace organization prides itself on presenting colorful, nonthreatening fare. However, large (sometimes very large) puppets—occasionally 3 or 4 feet tall—can startle little ones. Ever aware of this potential "fear" factor (particularly during Tot Wednesday and Thursday performances), puppeteers often introduce themselves before stepping behind the stage, and many come out again after the show to allow kids a closer look at the "cast." Shows last about 45 minutes. Most "performers" are hand puppets; however, the theater hosts occasional marionettes, rod and shadow puppets, and others.

KEEP IN MIND Daily shows are often given during schools' winter vacations, but show frequency diminishes in the summer. Because of its small size (95 seats), Puppet Showplace is frequently a sellout, so call for reservations. Since seating is unreserved, arrive early for the best choice, though there really isn't a bad seat in the house.

PURGATORY CHASM

It's only fitting that a place called purgatory should take you on a jagged path progressively downward. But despite its ominous moniker, this natural wonder is actually a slice of adventure heaven, a place accurately described by local rangers as a natural playground for kids. You'll travel about an hour from Boston to get here, but it's definitely worth the trip.

A find dating from the 18th century, the place got its name from the spooky aura created by towering rocks and thick, unwieldy brush (since removed by rangers). As for the origin of the chasm itself, experts are still debating it. An 18th-century villager swore it opened up overnight, but more scientific theories attribute it to earthquakes and glaciers.

On paper, the ¼-mile-long, 50-foot-wide chasm doesn't seem so vast. Inside is another story. Huge, craggy rocks jut out in all directions, requiring nimble feet—and unfettered hands—to navigate. The circuit is most definitely a challenge, and you'll need to be physically

KEEP IN MIND Remember three words: bring bandage strips. Though most kids manage the terrain with ease (and better than their parents), scrapes happen. You'll kick yourself if you're at the bottom of the chasm with a boo-booed, crying child. A bottle of water isn't a bad idea, either. Food, on the other hand, is prohibited in the chasm. Whatever you carry, put it in a backpack, because you'll need your hands to climb. And since it's 10° cooler at the bottom, bring a sweatshirt, although you're bound to work up a sweat on the climb.

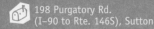

198 Purgatory Rd.
(I–90 to Rte. 146S), Sutton

 Free

Daily sunrise–sunset

508/234-3733 or 508/234-9610;
www.state.ma.us/dem/parks/purg.htm

5 and up

fit (not to mention nonclaustrophobic) to manage it. But don't be deterred by the beginning. Those first few steps are indeed some doozies, necessitating a little hands-and-knees maneuvering. But once you get past the Devil's Pulpit (those Puritans just loved those bedeviled titles), the going gets easier. The most popular trail takes you 1½ miles to the bottom of the chasm (70 feet down) and back; look for the blue paint that marks the trail. Take a hard left at Devil's Coffin or you'll veer off the rocks onto a rather ordinary wooded path. (A note to the adventurous and foolhardy: climbing the surrounding rock faces is strictly prohibited without a permit.) The faint of heart (and not everyone will feel comfortable climbing here) can still enjoy the view on the trails that run the chasm's perimeter. Skip the trails entirely in winter and wet weather, when slippery conditions make them unsafe. The 110-acre park also includes a picnic area, playground equipment, and, perhaps best of all, a shiny new visitor center with shiny new bathrooms you can use after you're done communing with nature.

EATS FOR KIDS

Picnic in the gazebo at the trail-head, where an ice-cream truck parks in summer. For more ice cream, hot dogs, soups, and snacks, cross Route 146 to **West End Creamery** (481 Purgatory Rd., Whitinsville, tel. 508/234–2022). In Sutton, **Blue Jay's** (489 Central Tpke., tel. 508/865–9955) serves comfort food.

HEY, KIDS! A lot of the chasm's landmarks have spooky names. Devil's Coffin, an above-ground cave you can actually go in, has a large, rectangular stone that looks like a vampire's coffin. Mother Nature even saw fit to include what looks like a headstone. Be sure to look for the old verse carved at the entrance: "Prepare to meet thy God." It looks to have been carved about 100 years ago, but no one knows its exact origins.

SALEM

No allusion to the American witch is complete without a reference to Salem. The quiet, seaside enclave was seemingly brimming with dark artists a few centuries ago. Back then, scads of young women were accused of practicing witchcraft, which led to the infamous Salem Witch Trials and made the town the best-known horror hamlet this side of Transylvania.

A surprise to most kids, the witches here have nothing to do with pointed black hats or twitching noses, a fact illustrated at the Salem Witch Museum (Washington Sq., tel. 978/744–1692). A good place to become oriented, the museum describes what really started the hysteria—basically an overreaction to teenage-girl rebellion—and how it led to the hangings of 19 of the accused. The Witch Dungeon Museum (16 Lunde St., tel. 978/741–3570) goes a few steps further, guiding visitors through its dungeons and re-creating

EATS FOR KIDS In a Pig's Eye (148 Derby St., tel. 978/741–4436) sounds inhospitable, but it serves renowned sandwiches, salads, pastas, desserts, and a few Mexican dishes. At **Victoria Station** (Pickering Wharf, tel. 978/745–3400), a huge menu with burgers and salads takes second place to the water view.

KEEP IN MIND Salem has more to offer than witchcraft. A short tour of Nathaniel Hawthorne's House of the Seven Gables (54 Turner St., tel. 978/744–0991) is mostly architectural, but a trip up the mysterious hidden staircase (it's narrow, so suck in your gut) is a thrill. See maritime history at the Salem Maritime National Historic Site (193 Derby St., tel. 978/740–1660). Explore ne'er-do-wells of the sea at the New England Pirate Museum (274 Derby St., tel. 978/741–2800) and two centuries of art and artifacts at the Peabody Essex Museum (East India Sq., tel. 800/745–4054). Pioneer Village (Forest River Park, tel. 978/744–0991) re-creates 1630s Salem.

Park service visitor center:
2 New Liberty St.

 Varies by attraction

877/SALEM MA; www.salem.org

 Many attractions Apr–Oct; days
and times vary

6 and up

the trial of Sarah Good. You can even "enjoy" the sight of the reconstructed gallows. Figurines (some of them grim) at the Salem Wax Museum (288 Derby St., tel. 800/298–2929) depict wayward seafarers as well as witches. Learn about the practice of real witchcraft at Salem Witch Village (282R Derby St., tel. 978/740–9229).

That Salem has embraced its mystical image is evidenced by such attractions as the Museum of Myths and Monsters (59 Wharf St., tel. 978/745–8383) and the Witch History Museum (197–201 Essex St., tel. 978/741–7770). The ghouls inside do not necessarily have to do with Colonial-era witches, but they do fit in with the creepy theme. The town becomes particularly magical in October, when haunted happenings include spooky houses, street fairs, and concerts (some events may be too scary for some kids).

HEY, KIDS! The hidden staircase in the House of the Seven Gables is something of a mystery. Though stories abound—it's been credited with every-thing from hiding young girls during the witch trials to being part of the Un-derground Railway—its true origins are unknown. It might simply have been the house's original staircase before the home was expanded to its current size. For the rest, you'll have to use your imagination.

You've got to hand it to Six Flags for their scare-your-pants-off contraptions. Roller coaster enthusiasts, start your engines: this ride emporium is rife with the stuff of thrill seekers' dreams.

Once upon a time, this was the family-owned Riverside Amusement Park, but the Massachusetts staple shed its mom-and-pop roots in 1996, when it was purchased by Premier Parks. Today the banner reads Six Flags (Premier Parks bought the mega-park operator), and the park now has name recognition and all the bells and whistles—and cartoon characters—to go with it.

Six Flags is known for its constitution-challenging assortment of rides, and the offerings here seem right in character. Like scary? Try Flashback, a high-speed jaunt that takes you turning and looping one way, and then does it all again—backwards. Then soar with the Man of Steel at speeds of up to 70 miles per hour on Superman—Ride of Steel. At 2½ minutes,

EATS FOR KIDS If you haven't lost your lunch on Superman (or if you have and you need to fill 'er up again), try the **Superhero Grill,** which has the requisite burgers and fries. In Movie Town, the **Commissary** has reasonably priced burgers and chicken—a big plate will run about $6, but the drink will tack on another $2—atop an enormous mound of fries, which may or may not be a good thing. Right across the street from the water park, **Cooks in the Kitchen** (1668 Main St., tel. 413/786–8068) offers burgers, sandwiches, fish-and-chips—and air-conditioning.

 1623 Main St., Agawam

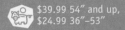 $39.99 54" and up, $24.99 36"–53"

 413/786-9300

Late Apr–late May and early Sept–Oct, Sa–Su 10–9; Memorial Day–Labor Day, approx daily 10–10 (hrs vary)

All ages

this baby is l-o-o-ng by roller coaster standards, screaming out of the starting gate with a 221-foot drop. It's New England's tallest, fastest, and longest coaster and is the focal point of a new 12-acre park section including such groovy restaurants as the DC Comics Diner (hint: eat *after* you ride). If all of this doesn't leave you a quivering hunk of mush, try out Scream, another of the self-explanatory monster thrill rides that have jump-started the park's transformation. Never one to rest on its laurels, the park has added new thrills in the form of Batman, the Dark Knight.

Thankfully, Six Flags has taken mercy on the less iron-gutted among us, offering lower-thrill fare as well. Poison Ivy's Twisted Train, for example, is billed as a family coaster. If you need to remove yourself from the big guns completely, try Tiny Timber Town or Looney Tunes Movie Town, a family area featuring rides and shows, as well as that Wascally Wabbit (AKA Bugs Bunny) and friends.

KEEP IN MIND
Surprisingly, Friday is often the least crowded day. Dress appropriately, as the cement landscape gets mighty hot and only one restaurant is air-conditioned. To cool off, visit the adjacent Island Kingdom water park (included in price). Discounted Late Gate admission is offered after 4.

GETTING THERE Though the directions aren't nearly as complicated as they may seem, make sure you have a copy with you. Take I–90 west to Exit 6, I–291 west. Travel 4⁹⁄₁₀ miles to I–91 south. Travel 2⁹⁄₁₀ miles to Exit 3. Cross the bridge and take the first exit. Follow the rotary to Route 57 west, then to Route 159 south, which is Main Street. Six Flags is 2⁹⁄₁₀ miles down on the left. Getting here from Boston will take a good 1½ hours, but that's better than a three-hour flight to another well-known park.

SKATER ISLAND

9

When parents talk, kids occasionally listen. When Tony Hawk talks, they definitely open their ears.

The preeminent skateboard guru has sung the praises of this cavernous indoor skating paradise, even launching it into virtual renown (*see* Hey, Kids!, *below*). Scads of local X-Games types have weighed in with their own opinions, too, showing up in droves since the park's 1998 opening and dubbing the indoor palace heaven on wheels.

Designed by a guy named Twister (would you expect anything else?), Skater Island feature's more than 20,000 square feet of terrain. That may seem less than giant next to some of the behemoths out west, but fans say that what it lacks in size, it more than makes up for with superior quality. Hit the ground in the pool (6-foot shallow end, 9-foot deep end, "with a foot of vert," if that means anything to you), street (featuring

HEY, KIDS!
Can't get to Skater Island today? Visit it at home. Tony Hawk Pro Skater™ 3 features the park at level 6.

KEEP IN MIND The trip from Boston will take you about 90 minutes, but you'll no doubt attain major hero status for the effort. Repeat visitors should consider a membership, which nets discounts on admission (M–F $8, Sa–Su $10) as well as entry to special events. Tony-Hawks-in-training should ask about Skater Island's annual summer camp.

1747 W. Main Rd. (Rte. 114),
Middletown, RI

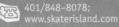 M–F $13, Sa–Su $15

 July–Aug, sessions daily 9–1, 1–5,
5–9; Sept–June, M–F 12–3, 3–6, 6–9;
Sa–Su 9–1, 1–5, 5–9

 401/848–8078;
www.skaterisland.com

the all-important ramps, quarter pipes, and hand rails), 12-foot-high vertical ramp, and 100-foot-long snake run. If the very idea of careening down such a thing gives you a headache, consider a lesson ($35 an hour), available by reservation a few days to a week ahead. Boarders and in-line skaters are welcome every day, though Tuesday and Sunday nights are limited to bikers only (freestyle bikes, for those out of the loop). Helmets are required. Don't have one? Headgear is available for rent ($5 fee, $20 deposit). Pads aren't required but are recommended.

Demos, contests, and other special events are regular island occurrences. Keep your eye out for appearances by the pros. About once a week someone tends to show up and skate right alongside the amateurs, spiking the excitement meter. Vicarious thrill seekers and the simply faint of heart can look out over the action from the overhead catwalks at no charge.

EATS FOR KIDS Food breaks between runs can be indulged via on-site vending machines or pizza delivery (ask staff for take-out menus). If you're eating out, dozens of the usual suspects can be found along Route 114, including **Chili's Grill & Bar** (845 W. Main Rd., tel 401/848–9380) and **Applebee's Neighborhood Grill** (349 W. Main Rd., tel. 401/849–5676).

SOUTH SHORE NATURAL SCIENCE CENTER

8

Lots of folks think you have to travel far to find interesting wild critters worth investigating. But Jeff Corwin, star and amiable explorer of his own eponymous Animal Planet show, says Massachusetts has plenty to offer. "Here in about three or four lakes in Southeastern Massachusetts, we have a turtle that is found nowhere else in the world," he says, referring to the Plymouth red-bellied turtle.

Little nature lovers will have a fine time sharing Corwin's passion for the South Shore ecosystem at this small institution focused entirely on local wetland habitats. The well-known naturalist found his love for all things scaly, furry, and otherwise at the center, and despite worldwide travels, he continues to find the South Shore pretty cool. In fact, he helped create the center's new EcoZone, a 3,000-square-foot space that's a miniature indoor version of the local world outside. Central to it is a small pond with several species of turtles and frogs. Crawl through the adjacent hollow tree (generously sized so adults can fit, too) for an underwater frog's-eye view. Future plans include a quaking bog, a phenomenon created

KEEP IN MIND Indoor exhibits are admittedly on the small side, so to fully appreciate the center, come on a nice day. Admission fees cover the indoor exhibits; trails are free of charge. Those with kids crying for souvenirs needn't be afraid of the gift shop, which has an unusually large supply of very inexpensive, nature-oriented trinkets. Check the center's large list of programs, which includes a summer camp.

Jacob's La. (Rte. 3 Exit 13), Norwell

 $5 ages 16 and up, $2.50 children 3–15

M–Sa 9:30–4:30

781/659-2559; www.ssnsc.org

2–12

by glacial activity (a real one is nearby at the fascinating Black Pond Hill Bog). Staff naturalists appear regularly, allowing kids to get close to such live residents as Bob the iguana and Hedwig the owl, who lives outside. Plants in the adjacent greenhouse include several local carnivorous species, such as the Cobra Lilly. Don't worry; they only eat bugs.

Six outdoor trails for all hiking levels let you explore the habitats firsthand. Try a Quest, an utterly absorbing nature walk in which you search for puzzle clues and locate a stashed box. The challenge is in identifying such things as turkey tail fungus. A Mini Quest takes no more than 30 minutes. If you like it, ask at the gift shop about the *South Shore Quests* book ($4). Sponsored by the Appalachian Mountain Club, it maps out the center's longer and more challenging Picture Quest, as well as more than a dozen other nearby South Shore quest adventures.

EATS FOR KIDS

Though the center feels sequestered, there are vast food choices nearby. On Route 23, **Friendly's** (1985 Washington St., tel. 781/878–7627) serves mountains of comfort food and ice cream. **Togo's Great Sandwiches** (2117 Washington St., tel. 781/659–7400) has particularly tasty versions of the obvious fare.

HEY, KIDS! Venus's-flytraps aren't the only predators that need meat to keep their leafy figures. According to Corwin, the lovely-looking pitcher plant lures its prey with a sweet liquid. "They fall into this bath of digestive juices, and then the plant gets the nutrition it needs." Even better, he adds, "Then it uses the stink of the decomposed animal to attract other flies."

SOUTHWICK'S ZOO

What do you do when you're an animal conservationist with a dairy farm? Sell the cattle and turn the place into a zoo. That's just what Justin Southwick did in 1952, transforming his 200-year-old homestead into a home for animals large and small. Today Southwick's has evolved into a full-fledged private zoo—purportedly New England's largest—with lions, tigers, bears, and all. There are about 500 unlikely beasts here, some endangered, some just plain cute. Though purists once balked at some of the smaller habitats (a result of the facility's 1950s origins), the zoo has recently taken great pains to bring their structures up-to-date (including lion and tiger habitats), and there's no question that Southwick's animals are well loved.

Close encounters are what set Southwick's apart. Animals here are accessible (the aforementioned lions, tigers, and bears notwithstanding). Giraffes are so close, you can almost look them in the eye—if, of course, they were to bend down over their fence, which they sometimes do. Elephants stand close enough for you to see how hairy

HEY, KIDS!

Certain species of tortoises rate as some of the earth's oldest creatures. Aldabra tortoises can live as long as 150 years. Both of Southwick's resident Aldabras are roughly 100 years old. Another surprising animal fact: rhino horns are not made out of ivory, but rather compressed hair.

EATS FOR KIDS With cozy benches and booths, homespun **Lowell's** (16 Hastings St., tel. 508/473–1073) looks positively old-time, and has comfort food to match. The enormous menu of sandwiches, salads, and seafood—even a "rooster" (fresh fried chicken) for kids should have something to please everyone. **New England Steak and Seafood** (11 Uxbridge Rd. [Rte. 16], tel. 508/473–5079) has a similarly vast menu but in a more formal, but still comfortable, atmosphere. Choices include pasta, seafood, and grills, as well as a large children's menu. The zoo itself has a couple of snack shacks.

2 Southwick St. (off Rte.16), Mendon

 508/883–9182 or 800/258–9182;
www.southwickzoo.com

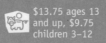 $13.75 ages 13
and up, $9.75
children 3–12

 May–Columbus Day, daily 10–5;
limited operation Apr and late Oct

All ages

they really are. For an extra charge, you can actually ride one of the big guys. The zoo offers camel and pony rides as well (weight restrictions apply for these). In the petting zoo, goats and sheep, including absolutely adorable kids and lambs, are more than happy to accept offerings of food from your kids and lambs (use the feed machines only, please). Don't bother trying to hide the pellets; these hungry hogs (figuratively speaking) will nibble right out of your pocket!

Look for chimps in a new naturalistic exhibit where moats—instead of fences—provide unfettered eye contact. One of the zoo's most unusual features and a definite highlight is the Deer Forest. Dozens of deer call this 35-acre, gated forest home. Grab a 25¢ fistful of feed from one of the machines and enjoy as the deer nibble directly from your hand. You could spend the better part of the day right here. After the animal adventures, go wild at the on-site playground or on the small collection of kiddie rides.

KEEP IN MIND Animal feeding is a wonderful thing as long as you're aware of the creatures' dispositions. Friendly (and hungry!) deer sometimes swarm food-toting visitors, a circumstance that, while not dangerous, can be frightening to a young child. Ask for a schedule of daily presentations about elephants, primates, and reptiles.

SPORTS MUSEUM OF NEW ENGLAND

New England fans still celebrating the kick heard round the world (Adam Vinitieri's Super Bowl–winning field goal) can pay homage to their football heroes—as well as the rest of the hometown teams—at this arena-side attraction.

Perched on the fifth floor of the shiny new sports arena (the one that replaced the Boston Garden in body, if not in local sports enthusiasts' hearts), this facility is a fan's dream. Though actual exhibit space numbers only about 10,000 square feet, the striking location, from which you can actually eyeball the Bruins' frozen rink and the Celtics' famous parquet floor, makes it seem much more impressive. Since the museum is closed on rare matinee-game days, come early on the day of a night game (around 10:30 AM), and you may even spot the home teams and visitors conducting their practice shoot- or skate-arounds.

Exhibits and memorabilia are spread over two levels. Look for displays on hockey, basketball, baseball, the Boston Marathon, and, of course, football (the museum hopes to add Vinitieri's

EATS FOR KIDS In addition to having great food, the **Fours** (166 Canal St., tel. 617/720– 4455) has nearly enough memorabilia to be considered a sports museum itself. At the **Commonwealth Fish & Beer** (138 Portland St., tel. 617/523–8383), you can enjoy pub fare while gazing at enormous brew tanks. And don't forget the North End, with all its incredible Italian restaurants and pastry shops.

1 FleetCenter

617/624-1234 recording, 617/624-1235 voice; www.sportsmuseum.org, www.fleetcenter.com

$6 ages 17 and up, $4 children 6–17

T–Sa 11–5, Su 12–5; admission on hr

10 and up

shoe to the display). Those who haven't gotten over the demise of the Garden can wax nostalgic in actual Boston Garden seats while watching a video on the grande dame, or imagine themselves sitting out a call for high sticking in a genuine Bruins penalty box. There's plenty more nostalgia at the ESPN kiosk, where you can call up footage of the 100 greatest sports moments. Two highlights: the 1980 U.S. Olympic hockey victory and hometown hero Doug Flutie's Hail Mary pass in the Cotton Bowl. Another ESPN exhibit lets you try your skill at a sports anchor desk.

There are a few interactive games as well. The mitts-down favorite is the Roger Clemens catch. In this virtual game, you catch a strikeout and actually feel the "thump" of the ball as it "falls" into your mitt. The Rocket also dispenses a few tidbits about his form (spitting not included). While you're here, look for computer hookups to various Internet sports sites.

KEEP IN MIND

The museum occasionally closes down—during sound checks on concert days, for example—so call ahead. As parking is often a nightmare, opt for public transportation (the Green Line's North Station) when you can. Drivers should use the relatively economical MBTA lot under the FleetCenter.

HEY, KIDS! Zambonis weren't always so easy to use. Before they became motorized in the 1930s, ice groomers took the form of horse-drawn scrapers followed by attendants who spread hot water over the ice. (The hot water would fill the cracks and freeze in a smoother sheet.) Because the process was so cumbersome, it was only done once per hockey game (as opposed to twice, as it is today). And in case you're wondering, the horses did not wear skates.

SWAN BOATS AT THE PUBLIC GARDEN

You know it's spring in Boston when the swans come back to town. Not the real birds (although those are here, too), but the oversize floating entities known as the Swan Boats. Fixtures in Boston for more than 100 years, these graceful birds migrate back to the Public Garden each April, giving thousands of delighted passengers perfectly serene jaunts around the famous lagoon.

Set afloat in 1877 by entrepreneur Robert Paget, the watercraft have become a symbol of the complete Boston experience. Paget's idea was simply to provide a novel diversion. The concept for the swan came out of the need to camouflage the mechanism for locomotion, in this case a human-propelled paddle wheel. And talk about low-tech! Fifteen-minute lagoon tours are made possible only through the efforts of some very energetic crewmen (one per boat), who motor the 20-passenger vehicles by pedaling.

KEEP IN MIND Because they're operated by humans, the Swan Boats are docked during especially rainy, windy, and hot days. Look for the real (feathered) swans to arrive back at the lagoon in late spring.

EATS FOR KIDS *Cheers* fans will recognize the exterior of the **Bull & Finch Pub** (84 Beacon St., tel. 617/227–9605) as the place where everybody knows your name. There's no Norm or Cliff, but there's plenty of above-average pub fare to fill you up. It is somewhat pricey, however; this is, after all, a tourist attraction. For another local suggestion, see the Boston Common.

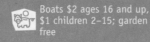
That the setting is the Public Garden makes the adventure all the more peaceful. Far more formal than its sibling (the Boston Common) across Charles Street, the manicured garden is decidedly more of a keep-off-the-grass kind of place (don't even think about bringing the Frisbee). Nevertheless, the 24-acre parcel, the nation's first public botanical garden, has its own charms, namely hundreds of species of flora. Well-marked paths pass by all of the prized plantings, and spring blooms make the garden a tapestry of color. All of this may well be lost on little ones, who would just as soon make a beeline to that homage to mallard-dom, the Duckling Sculpture. Bronze casts commemorate the fictional exploits of the *Make Way for Ducklings* clan (*see* #27). Feel free to climb on them; just don't take them home. (Despite having their webbed feet sunk in cement, the quackers have been the occasional victims of duck-nappers.)

HEY, KIDS! A few centuries ago, before dirt was carted in as fill, Boston was but a square mile surrounded by water. The blooming turf that is the Public Garden was a patch of salt marsh, and if you were where FAO Schwarz now is, you'd have been swimming.

U.S.S. CONSTITUTION

4

Old Ironsides doesn't sound like a nickname befitting a lady, but then this is no ordinary lady. Boston's grande dame of the sea, the U.S.S. *Constitution* achieved fame—not to mention its sturdy nickname—during the War of 1812, when its thick skin reportedly deflected a cannonball fired by the British frigate H.M.S. *Guerriere*. Nearly 200 years later, the old girl is still alive and kicking, currently the world's oldest commissioned warship still afloat.

In 1997, the historic vessel set the nautical world abuzz when it hoisted anchor and sailed out of the harbor for the first time in more than 100 years. These days you're more likely to see it docked than set to sea.

Thirty-minute guided tours of the vessel are led by active navy personnel who take you to two of the ship's lower decks for a look at how 19th-century sailors bunked, ate, slept, and went to war. It's pretty impressive when you realize that anywhere between 400 and

HEY, KIDS! Some of the youngest sailors aboard the *Constitution* were called "powder monkeys." These quick and agile crewmen—some as young as 8, but mostly young teens—carried gunpowder during battles, running from the ship's bottom (where the powder was stored) up several decks to the guns. Guns had to be reloaded after every firing. Not only was the job exhausting, it was dangerous. Since they were essential to artillery operation, powder monkeys were often the targets of enemy fire. Alas, if you were a boy who wanted to go to sea, this was the only job in town.

Charlestown Navy Yard,
Charlestown

Free

617/242-5601 ship, 617/426-1812
museum; www.ussconstitution.navy.mil

Tours daily 10-4; museum May-Oct,
daily 9-6; Nov-Apr, daily 10-5

All ages

500 men shared these cramped quarters for 12 months at a time. But then, as a guide points out, the ship was built for war, not for pleasure cruising.

To fully appreciate the ship's legacy, you'll want to stop by the Constitution Museum. The three-story structure details the life of the vessel and its men through artifacts, such as ship's logs, journals, and sailor gear. Kid-friendly highlights include some interactive devices through which 19th-century sailing gets a 21st-century twist. A ship's wheel, for example, is attached to a computer screen that lets you navigate into war position, and virtual ammunition can be fired from the barrel of a real cannon. Anyone who has wondered how they get ships into those little bottles can visit the model makers' studios and maybe try their hand at fashioning a model themselves. (Check with the front desk on your way in for studio times.)

KEEP IN MIND
To complete your nautical experience, visit the U.S.S. *Cassin Young*, also in the Charlestown Navy Yard. In its heyday, the WWII destroyer packed anti-aircraft, anti-submarine, and anti-ship weaponry.

EATS FOR KIDS In summer, the **Shipyard Galley** (Bldg. 10, Pier 1, tel. 617/241-5660), opposite the ship, serves burgers and snacks. **Tavern on the Water** (1 Pier 6, 8th St., tel. 617/242-8040) provides good food year-round—from broiled seafood and burgers to a large children's menu plus stellar spots for watching the ships.

WALDEN POND

Don't even bother bringing the cell phone to this peaceable pond. It probably won't work, but even if it did, you'd be missing the whole point. Massachusetts's most famous pond, after all, is nothing if not a place to get away from it all.

Though the esteemed swimming hole is still a retreat, it isn't quite as secluded as it used to be. Visible from the main road, Walden Pond is just steps from the corner of Routes 2 and 126. Miraculously, though, when you're down at the water's edge, it feels sequestered just the same, somehow retaining the idyllic aura that inspired Henry David Thoreau to pen a book in its name.

Thoreau took up residence on the pond in 1845, on a lot owned by friend Ralph Waldo Emerson. Holed up for two years in his one-room cabin (a replica of which stands near the parking lot), the writer communed with nature and wrote, ultimately publishing

EATS FOR KIDS Good, reasonably priced food in this touristy neighborhood isn't an easy find. At **Papa Razzi** (768 Elm St., tel. 978/371–0030), you'll find pizzas, pastas, salads, and kid fare. The **Ninety-Nine Restaurant** (13 Commonwealth Ave., tel. 978/ 369–0300) has pages of burgers, salads, soups, and other dishes.

KEEP IN MIND Walden's inherent charms are the good news; its over-popularity is the bad. Balmy weather can bring tens of thousands here. In order to protect the environment, rangers keep a tight lid on capacity (1,000 people max), turning away carloads of disappointed wannabe swimmers. To ensure a spot on the sand, arrive early on those hot summer days. Pets, fires, and motorized watercraft are prohibited. The park offers seasonal activities, including children's crafts, story times, and tours. Look outside the Walden shop or call the main number for information.

Visitor center: 915 Walden St.
(Rte. 126, near Rte. 2), Concord

 Parking $5
per vehicle

 Daily 8–sunset

978/369-3254

All ages

his experiences in the 1854 book *Walden: or, Life in the Woods.* The preservation of Thoreau's beloved land has become a cause célèbre for some of today's luminaries.

Though myriad four-legged animals—squirrels, rabbits, chipmunks, among others—continue to inhabit the area, it's the two-legged creatures that keep the place hopping. The fresh, clear water attracts more than a half million recreators annually, who come to swim, boat, picnic, or just to soak up the sun and scenery. Hiking is a year-round pastime; a scenic path runs 1⁸⁄₁₀ miles around the pond, and there are a total of 411 acres in the entire Walden Pond State Reservation. Anglers are often up to their waders with rod and reel, and cross-country skiers take to the trails in winter. But despite all these visitors and all this activity, nobody has explained why such a big body of water—what looks like a lake to the untrained eye—is called a pond.

HEY, KIDS! Though Thoreau made it famous, Walden has a history that stretches back far before the author's days. Purportedly, the pond was formed 12,000 years ago by the last New England glacier, a thawing chunk of which broke off and melted into this 103-foot "kettle hole." How did the pond get its name? There are lots of theories, one of which has it that "Walden" is a consolidation of "walled in," which describes the ridges enclosing the pond. Then again, it's just a theory.

WESTON SKI TRACK

What to do with a snow-covered golf course during the dead of winter? How about turning it into a cross-country skiing center? A couple of entrepreneurs came up with this brilliant idea in 1975, harnessing the grounds of a public golf course and grooming it for cross-country skiers. While it's true that cross-country enthusiasts (those with their own equipment anyway) can ski for free virtually anywhere there's open space, what sets the Weston track apart is its conveniences. Groomed trails are a plus, especially for beginners. Snowmaking machines operate from late November through February, ensuring at least a little rural activity even when Mother Nature isn't cooperating. Equipment rental is available right on site. And where else can a family of four experience skiing (skis included!) for just about $60?

Nearly 10 miles of trails cover the entire golf course, though the track gets significantly smaller when there's no natural snow (snowmaking capabilities seem limited to the area nearest the lodge). Nevertheless, even then there's plenty to be entertaining.

KEEP IN MIND The golf-course terrain doesn't require a thick layer of snow, so don't count the place out just because you don't have a foot in your backyard. Just call ahead if you're wondering. Even in cold weather, you can work up a sweat, so to be comfortable throughout your adventure, dress in layers that can be easily removed and tied around your waist. To keep feet warm and dry while snowshoeing, wear a pair of durable, waterproof hiking boots. Those with extra gear to stow can bring a lock and use any of the lockers in the ski rental room.

 200 Park Rd., Weston

 $11 ages 13 and up, $6 children 6–12

Dec–Feb or as snow permits, M–Th 10–9:30, F 10–8, Sa 9–8, Su 9–6

 781/891–6575; www.ski-paddle.com/skitrack/skitrack.shtml

4 and up

Rental skis are stocked for kids as young as 3. Reasonably priced lessons are offered to those age 4 and up. If your tykes are too little to get around on their own two feet, you can rent a PULK (a gizmo that looks like a sled version of those three-wheeled trailers that attach to bicycles) and tow them along behind you. For something completely different, you can suit up the family in snowshoes, also available for rent.

The Weston's trails are relatively flat, so beginners need not worry about racing out of control. The more adventurous will find at least a few small hills. Veterans say the full circuit can be experienced in a couple of hours, but you may want to stick around. Night lights let you continue your adventure for several hours after sunset.

EATS FOR KIDS

The on-site **café** offers the all-important hot chocolate as well as hot dogs, soup, and snacks. If you'd like to warm up with some pizza or pasta, try **Papa Razzi** (16 Washington St., Wellesley, tel. 781/235–4747).

HEY, KIDS! Think cross-country is a snooze? Think again. Traditional cross-country skiing (what's called classical skiing) isn't the only way to travel. The new wave is "skate skiing," a method named for its skatinglike motion. You'll move a bit faster and still get some exercise. To give it a go, ask for "skates" when you rent (they're slightly different from regular skis), and stick to the specially groomed runs next to the traditional cross-country tracks. By the way, both styles are contested at the Olympics, so if you practice really hard . . .

WOLF HOLLOW

You wouldn't think an animal as seemingly common as a wolf could be endangered, but it is. Despite its familiar name, wolves have dwindled significantly in numbers (the result of early 20th-century efforts to save farm livestock) and are all but gone in 47 of the 50 states. Though the statistic pretty much negates the possibility of encountering a wolf in the wild, you'll get the next best thing at this unique, nonprofit animal habitat.

Dedicated entirely to educating people about wolves and how to preserve them, the facility gets visitors close to a pack in its natural habitat, providing a rare glimpse into the work-and-play life of these wild canines. The animals can be viewed from just outside a 1½-acre enclosure. From a few feet away, you'll be able to appreciate the personalities and appearances of the nine-member pack: the bearlike good looks of Denali, the graying coat of Geniek, or perhaps even the underbite of Lakota. While you observe, staff members detail the habits of these regal creatures and point out the significance of their behaviors.

HEY, KIDS!

Wolf packs have a distinct pecking order, and humans are at the bottom of it. To approach the pack, owner Joni Soffron must show her respect by crouching and avoiding eye contact with the alpha female. Otherwise she risks a reprimand: a stern stare and a grab.

KEEP IN MIND Wolf puppies come into the world in the second week in May (though not every year), and the little guys begin making public appearances when they're about two weeks old. To stand any chance of seeing the small pups, plan your visit for late May or June. For another type of wildlife adventure, check out Crane Beach/Crane Wildlife Refuge (Argilla Rd., tel. 978/356–4351). The shallow waters and climbing rocks of Wingaersheek Beach (Gloucester, tel. 978/281–9790) are a family favorite.

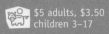

Wolf packs, it turns out, aren't all that different from human families. Each pack has a mother and father (the alpha female and male), who are the leaders. Siblings engage in rivalry (just watch as yearling Jelly picks on her brother Weeble), and children and subordinates show their respect by bowing when a parent enters. (OK, so they're not exactly like humans.) Once grown, pack members are assigned a job, such as hunting or puppy sitting. Performing the appointed task is crucial, says Joni Soffron, owner of Wolf Hollow. "If you don't do your job," she says, "you get kicked out of the pack."

Hour-long programs end with a group howl. Staff members counsel you on the correct pitch. If you're on key, you just may get the wolves to howl back.

EATS FOR KIDS Locals say the **Clam Box** (246 High St., tel. 978/ 356–9707) has the best fried clams in the East; however, the restaurant is closed December–February. For a large selection of burgers, salads, and such, head to the popular **Choate Bridge Pub** (3 S. Main St., tel. 978/356–2931).

CLASSIC GAMES

"I SEE SOMETHING YOU DON'T SEE AND IT IS BLUE." Stuck for a way to get your youngsters to settle down in a museum? Sit them down on a bench in the middle of a room and play this vintage favorite. The leader gives just one clue—the color—and everybody guesses away.

"I'M GOING TO THE GROCERY..." The first player begins, "I'm going to the grocery and I'm going to buy... " and finishes the sentence with the name of an object, found in grocery stores, that begins with the letter "A." The second player repeats what the first player has said, and adds the name of another item that starts with "B." The third player repeats everything that has been said so far and adds something that begins with "C" and so on through the alphabet. Anyone who skips or misremembers an item is out (or decide up front that you'll give hints to all who need 'em). You can modify the theme depending on where you're going that day, as "I'm going to X and I'm going to see..."

FAMILY ARK Noah had his ark—here's your chance to build your own. It's easy: Just start naming animals and work your way through the alphabet, from antelope to zebra.

PLAY WHILE YOU WAIT

NOT THE GOOFY GAME Have one child name a category. (Some ideas: first names, last names, animals, countries, friends, feelings, foods, hot or cold things, clothing.) Then take turns naming things that fall into that category. You're out if you name something that doesn't belong in the category—or if you can't think of another item to name. When only one person remains, start again. Choose categories depending on where you're going or where you've been—historic topics if you've seen a historic sight, animal topics before or after the zoo, upside-down things if you've been to the circus, and so on. Make the game harder by choosing category items in A-B-C order.

DRUTHERS How do your kids really feel about things? Just ask. "Would you rather eat worms or hamburgers? Hamburgers or candy?" Choose serious and silly topics—and have fun!

Build a Story "Once upon a time there lived..." Finish the sentence and ask the rest of your family, one at a time, to add another sentence or two. Bring a tape recorder along to record the narrative—and you can enjoy your creation again and again.

GOOD TIMES GALORE

WIGGLE & GIGGLE Give your kids a chance to stick out their tongues at you. Start by making a face, then have the next person imitate you and add a gesture of his own—snapping fingers, winking, clapping, sneezing, or the like. The next person mimics the first two and adds a third gesture, and so on.

JUNIOR OPERA During a designated period of time, have your kids sing everything they want to say.

THE QUIET GAME Need a good giggle—or a moment of calm to figure out your route? The driver sets a time limit and everybody must be silent. The last person to make a sound wins.

HIGH FIVES

BEST IN TOWN
Museum of Science
Children's Museum of Boston
New England Aquarium
George's Island
Old Sturbridge Village

BEST OUTDOORS
George's Island

WACKIEST
Davis' Mega Maze

BEST CULTURAL ACTIVITY
DeCordova Museum and Sculpture Park

NEW & NOTEWORTHY
Curious Creatures Kid'Zoo

BEST MUSEUM
Harvard Museum of Natural History

SOMETHING FOR EVERYONE

ART ATTACK
ArtBeat 66
DeCordova Museum and Sculpture Park 45
Museum of Fine Arts 25
Plaster Fun Time 16

FARMS AND ANIMALS
Blue Hills Trailside Museum and Reservation 64
Boston Harbor Cruises Whale Watching 60
Butterfly Place 54
Curious Creatures Kid'Zoo 48
Davis' Farmland 47
Drumlin Farm 41
Franklin Park Zoo 36
New England Aquarium 22
Plimoth Plantation 15
Southwick's Zoo 7
Wolf Hollow 1

FOOD FIXATION
Boston Tea Parlour 58
Faneuil Hall 38

FREEBIES
Boston Common 62
Castle Island Park 53
Community Solar System Trail 49
Dr. Paul Dudley White Bike Path 42
Faneuil Hall 38
Freedom Trail 35
Minute Man National Historical Park 26
Purgatory Chasm 12
Walden Pond 3

GAMES AND AMUSEMENTS
Davis' Mega Maze 46
Six Flags New England 10

GOOD SPORTS
Archery USA 68
Boulder Morty's 56
Charles River Canoe and Kayak 52
Community Boating 50
Dr. Paul Dudley White Bike Path 42
Fenway Park Tour 37

ALL AROUND TOWN

MANY THANKS!

A thousand thank-yous go to PR people all over the city, as well as the folks at the Greater Boston Convention & Visitors Bureau. My thanks to Nancy Holland, Jennifer Moore, Karen Lion, Anne Guthro, and all of my "road testers" at the McGovern and Memorial schools: Nathan, Holly, Emily, Ian, Dylan, Alex, Michael, Kasey, Trevor, Felicia, Kathryn, Bradley, Alex, Hillary, Ali, Michael, Thomas, Joseph, Leigha, Ashlee, Cara, Brian, David, Nicholas, Taylor, Olivia, Angela, Matthew, Kyle, Daniel, Jenna, Joshua, Andrew, Jennifer, Adria, Brittany, Christina, Alison, Tyler, Hannah, Leanne, Taha, Manuel, Andrew, Thomas, Christopher, Andrea, Elise, not to mention all of Girl Scout troop 4908. Thanks to all the Medway moms who shared their great ideas. My undying gratitude to my patient, wise, and eternally good-humored editor—did I mention patient?—Andrea Lehman. And finally, to my family—Steve, Alexis, and Melissa—who have followed me along on endless escapades, always with a smile. I wouldn't have missed a minute.

—Lisa Oppenheimer

the end